MARYADA PURUSHOTTAM THE MAKING OF MAN

A SON REMEMBERS

N. SRINIVASA RAGHAVAN

Contents

Prologue

In the Hinduism world view, yugas are cyclical time periods which demarcate different stages of evolution of human civilization. These ages are Krita (Satya) Yuga, Treta Yuga, Dvapara Yuga, and Kali Yuga. On the opposite ends of this time continuum are the Satya Yuga that represents the acme of human thought and conduct, and Kali Yuga that represents an age where righteousness is on the decline and unrighteousness is on the ascendant. In between these two are the Treta Yuga, and the Dvapara Yuga, which represent evolving stages of human consciousness, albeit at a progressively lesser level compared to the peak of human consciousness, which is Satya Yuga.

At present, we are in the Kali Yuga. And the Hindu world view stands vindicated, for we are living in an age where unrighteousness prevails over righteousness, untruth over truth, deception and hypocrisy over honesty, and disquiet and turbulence over peace. Given this bleak scenario, a fleeting thought that may cross the mind of a person with a very optimistic disposition is whether it is possible to come across someone in the Kali Yuga who carries with him a highly evolved consciousness that resonates with either the Satya Yuga or the Krita Yuga.

Lord Vishnu's incarnations correspond to these different yugas, and their purpose being to destroy unrighteousness and reestablish righteousness or Dharma. In the Treta Yuga, an incarnation of Vishnu that represented the acme of human thought and conduct was Lord Rama. He was the ideal son, the ideal brother, the ideal husband, and the ideal king who ruled over his kingdom. His entire life was a reiteration of nobility, dignity and propriety of human conduct, earning him the title of Maryada Purushottam, broadly translating to the noblest and the best among men.

Is it possible therefore for someone to come across a person in the Kali Yuga of today who tried to live his life by the ideals set forth by Lord Rama in the Treta Yuga. According to me, it is not all doom and gloom in the Kali Yuga. In my life of close to sixty years so far, I have had the privilege of observing and being with someone who epitomized Lord Rama in the way he conducted the different facets of his illustrious life of ninety years. Incidentally, his Ishta happened to be Lord Rama, and his admiration for his Ishta would pour forth in his conversations, particularly with me. He was an ideal son, an ideal brother, an ideal husband, an ideal father, an ideal employee, and above all an ideal human being.

My heart swells with pride in telling my readers that this person is none other than my dear father. And I am unequivocally setting forth here for the whole world to hear that it was my privilege to be born to such virtuous parents. And since the subject of this memoir is my father, my mother having predeceased him, the focus of this book will be my father.

One quality that I learnt from my illustrious father was in cultivating objectivity when seeing and judging anything. And it is this objective assessment, and not any filial bond that makes me say that at least as far as I am concerned, in my sixty years of having met people and observed them keenly, I have seen none more noble, more upright, more generous, more truthful, and more compassionate than my father.

To the entire world, Lord Rama is the very embodiment of Maryada Purushottam, including my dear father. But for me, my Maryada Purushottam is my dear father, and it is to my Maryada Purushottam that this book is dedicated. I am hopeful that readers will find this memoir engaging and inspiring.

Pranaams

Srinivasa Raghavan (Balu to my dear father)

My Father's Aaraadhya Maryada Purushottam Shri Ram

My Father My Hero

Safe and Secure in My Father's Arms

A Doting Father

My earliest memories of my father go back to the time when I was five or six years old. This was the turn of the 70s. I had already started attending school. We were three siblings; the eldest was my late elder brother, next was my sister, and I was the youngest. Since my father placed a very high premium on education, he got us all admitted to adjacent missionary schools, which were among the best in Hyderabad at that time, and which placed emphasis on all round development of the child.

All three of us would travel to school by bus. And on occasions when the school bus wouldn't turn up, my father would kickstart his Lambretta scooter, and all three of us of would be ferried to school with my sister and my brother sharing the rear seat, and I standing in front.

Since my father himself had had his education in a missionary school in Vijayawada, he took particular interest in ensuring that all three of us developed a good handwriting, our skills in the English language were reasonably good, and that we scored particularly well in Mathematics. While my elder brother and elder sister never disappointed my father in their Math score, I kind of disappointed him by being above average in mathematics.

My father and my uncle lived together as a joint family for close to eight years. And a special bond ensued with my cousins, my uncle's children. His first two children were both daughters, the elder one being Pratibha, and the younger one Priya. His son Guruvayurappan wasn't born during this joint family arrangement. My father doted on his two nieces, and we were one big, happy, simple, middle-class family.

Of all the children at home, I was the one who never disappointed anyone when it came to eating. My father loved to indulge any child who ate with a lot of relish. Every month, he would visit a general store by the name Society Stores on Bank Street, Hyderabad to buy our monthly quota of toiletries. The store also stocked up on lot of confectioneries, and I would accompany my father on these monthly visits to the store. Once there, I would typically request for biscuits shaped like animals, and a mouth freshener and a digestive prepared using fennel seeds, which gave the appearance of multicoloured rice grains packed in a plastic container shaped like a fish. After finishing with our purchases at Society Store, we would stop at a street food vendor opposite Koti Terminus, and have pani-poori, and once done, we would head to the Koti Maternity Hospital bus stop to catch our bus home. The store, which was such an integral part of my childhood couldn't withstand the vicissitudes of time. As I pass by the place where it once stood, it brings back nostalgic memories of the time I and Dad would make our monthly sojourns to the store. There are two other branches of the store that still continue under the name of Kathiawar Stores. One on Abid Road, sells lingerie, and the other one in Secunderabad sells dry fruits.

Once a month, my father would take us to Havemore Restaurant. And there, he would teach me etiquette, and table manners, as his little boy waited restlessly for his food to arrive. Havemore Restaurant have reinvented themselves as Ohris, with many more branches in the city today. But the simple ambience that it once provided to middle-class families has now given way to more spit and polish adding to its decorum, while at the same time adding up the price of the dishes that once seemed affordable and within the reach of the average middle-class family.

I would eagerly look forward to my summer vacations, as I could fully indulge my love for cricket, bicycling, and reading Amar Chitra Katha comics without a care in the world, and not having to worry about school assignments. I was fortunate enough to belong to a generation when we would be promoted to the next standard after the conclusion of our annual exams. New lessons for the new class wouldn't begin until after the completion of the summer vacations. So, the prospect of some lessons for the next standard being taught, and homework given to us to be done during the summer vacation just wasn't there. So, summer vacations meant not having to look at my school bag for a full two months.

Summer vacations also meant mango time. The markets would be awash with different varieties of mangoes, and my father himself greatly relished eating a whole mango. And he ensured that the love for the king of the fruits was passed down to his children as well, particularly me. So, he would buy a few kilograms of mangoes, wash them, and soak them in a bucket of water with ice in it, so as to allow the mangoes to chill. We didn't have the luxury of a refrigerator at home, and this was the substitute mechanism that would come into play for cooling the mangoes. And he taught us how to eat a whole mango without dropping a bit of pulp or juice on the ground.

Every new academic season meant a new pair of uniforms, new black shoes from Batas. We would head to the Bata Stores on Chikkadpally main road, and I remember once my father getting me black shoes with a compass embedded in the heel in one of the shoes. These shoes cost a princely sum of Rs. 32/- then. And the shoes with the compass was one of my prized childhood possessions.

We moved to Delhi in the summer of 1975, as Dad joined Hydrocarbons India Ltd., a wholly-owned subsidiary of Oil and Natural Gas Commission (ONGC). Dad had taken up a nice large, old-fashioned accommodation in East Patel Nagar, exactly at the point where East Patel Nagar ended, and the upward sloping road from our house onwards led to West Patel Nagar. Every Sunday, Dad would take all of us to explore Ajmal Khan Road, and Karol Bagh, the major shopping areas of West Delhi. It was during these outings that Dad introduced us to vegetarian North Indian cuisine.

Every Sunday, on East Patel Nagar main market, the proprietor of Radha Swamy Chaat Bhandaar based at Old Rajinder Nagar would set up his stall in the market to sell chhole. His preparation was so delicious that it would get sold out in minutes. I and Dad would walk down to the market with a stainless-steel utensil into which he would pour as many plates or portions of chhole that we wished to purchase. He would top it off with beautifully sliced onion rings and give it to us. This was an era when the scourge of plastics and takeaways hadn't yet started. I have to say that since then, I haven't tasted such lovely chhole. God bless the soul whose culinary skills and talents were simply divine.

We would walk down to Ajmal Khan Road, and the road stretched straight and long for close to two kilometers, starting from the Pusa road end, intersected midway by Arya Samaj Road, and going on till Deshbandu Gupta Marg. It was on the second stretch of Ajmal Khan Road starting from the Arya Samaj Road intersection that father would take us to a sweet shop cum restaurant (that's the trend in Delhi) called Kailash

Restaurant, and it is there I remember Dad treating us to Chhole-bature, tikkis, samosas, lassi and the like. At other times, we would walk down to the West Patel Nagar market, where all of us would be treated to mango shake in summers. These are memories of nearly fifty years ago, and they are fresh even as I write them down now, rendered precious and priceless because of dad.

A Strict Disciplinarian

When it came to our academic performance, and our general behaviour in our extended family get-togethers and in our neighbourhood, he was very particular about our academic grades, and our general behaviour. While my elder brother and sister were very studious, and well-behaved, it was I who needed disciplining as I was a playful, happy go lucky soul, and given to boyhood mischiefs.

Once, a complaint came from our neighbours that I had made faces at them. The spanking that began right in front of them continued even after we had returned home. And mom being a wise woman, never intervened. In hindsight, I believe it was all a necessary part of growing up.

My father was very particular about my math score. This was an area where my scores would just be above average, and didn't set my report card on fire, figuratively speaking. So, the day I would get my report card, I would have an early dinner, and pretend to be asleep. Dad would come in a little late from office (work meant worship for him), and while having dinner, enquire from mom about my report card. She would reply in the affirmative, and tell him that I was asleep, while all the while, I would be eavesdropping on their conversation. In the morning, as I was getting ready to go to school, I would just sneak in my report card before him for his signature. He would lovingly sign it, and I would be off to school. I am sure he must have known what I was up to, but chose to look the other way.

During our summer vacations, typically from Class III to Class VI, he would insist that I write a page of transcription (the subject should be an article from the Editorial Column that I should first read, then understand, and finally write). Apart from this, I had to solve ten Math problems. Though I wasn't too particular about these summer assignments, some of it did have an effect in later years. Beginning Class IX, I developed a love for Mathematics, and developed a very good handwriting modeled on the lines of my father's handwriting. And reading the newspaper became a lifelong habit that continues till today. I dedicate a full chapter later on how he sharpened my mathematical skills.

Another incident that I need to mention was the very important lesson he taught me of not signing any document without thoroughly reading it. The time must have been sometime in 1980 when I was in Class XI. We (my elder brother, elder sister and me) were all taught to do household chores from the tender age of ten. I was in my sixteenth year then. It was a Sunday, and one of dad's friends had come calling. He was his colleague. So, dad asked me to step out and buy sugar from the Fair Price Shops. This was the era of the command and control economy, which instead of ushering in a more egalitarian order, bred corruption of unimaginable proportions. Food rations were distributed through Fair Price Shops by the Food Corporation of India to citizens who had ration cards. The quantum of rice, wheat, and sugar was determined based on the size of the family. Middle class families who had a ration card chose to forego their wheat and rice rations, as they were of poor quality, and chose to buy only sugar, as sugar happened to be a coveted commodity in the open market.

Fair Price Shop owners would then unscrupulously sell the unclaimed wheat and rice in the open market at inflated prices. I went down to the designated Fair Price Shop in our area, and asked for sugar. He made out a bill to be paid for the sugar that we were entitled to. I paid him the amount and walked home. As I entered the hall where dad was still engaged in a conversation with his friend, he asked me to show him the bill. As he saw the bill, his first reaction to me was "Son, are you an uneducated and illiterate person?". He said this right in front of his friend. He then called me over, and showed me the mischief the Fair Price Shop owner had indulged in. He had billed for the wheat and rice that we were entitled to, but didn't chose to buy. By signing this bill, I had provided him a clear alibi that he had indeed sold us our entitled quota of rice and wheat, which he did not. So, in a way, I had unwittingly played a part in the FPS owner perpetrating a fraud. That was when my father sternly advised me never ever to sign a document before having first read it thoroughly, and understood its contents. That lesson has stayed with me ever since.

A couple of years down the line, he took on the role of my friend, philosopher, and guide when the changes and challenges of adolescence so overwhelmed and confused me that it dragged me down into a downward spiral of depression, despondency and self-doubt. In a later chapter, I will talk at length of this very critical role that my father played in my life that helped me confront my inner demons, and prepared me for much sterner tests that life was to present me with.

Broadening Horizons

Another important assignment during summer vacations was to read the English classics. He knew that reading classics would bring in greater emotional maturity, and improve our vocabulary and our language. But the child in me was more interested in reading Amar Chitra Katha comics, Phantom, Mandrake, Flash Gordon, and Tarzan comics. From comics, I graduated to adventure stories of Enid Blyton (Famous Five, Secret Seven et al), Franklin W Dixon (the adventures of Frank and Joe Hardy), and The Three Investigators (Jupiter Jones, Bob Andrews, and Pete Crenshaw).

After persistent coaxing from my father, the first classics I moved on to was reading Arthur Conan Doyle's collection of fifty-two short stories, and four novels of the one and only Sherlock Holmes. The character of Sherlock Holmes so captured my boyhood imagination that he continues to fascinate me even today. Therefore, when I got an opportunity, I requested my cousin who was visiting US on an official assignment to procure me the entire boxed set of Sherlock Holmes DVDs, the titular role enacted brilliantly by the late Jeremy Brett. No portrayal of Holmes comes even remotely close to the nuanced portrayal of Holmes by Jeremy Brett, who brought out the character exactly as Conan Doyle had created it.

In my second year of college, I had chosen English as one of my elective subjects. I had to go through the university abridged editions of Tess of the D'urbervilles by Thomas Hardy, and Great Expectations by Charles Dickens. Rather than seek the easier option out, I brought the original of both the classics and read them. Reading these classics not only improved my vocabulary, and helped me appreciate the style of writing of these celebrated authors, but also left a deep impression on me, and helped me evolve into a better person.

Keeping ourselves updated on General Knowledge was another key area that my father paid particular attention to. Knowing the capitals of almost every country, different currencies of different countries, names of Parliaments of different countries had a quick recall. Our time was the time of the radio, and I would assiduously follow the Bournvita Quiz contest on radio every Sunday, and also Quiz Time on television. And as I grew up, a natural inclination to get a pulse on the politics of the country in particular, and the world in general also developed. He would make it a point to bring home Time magazine and Newsweek magazine from office, and I remember browsing through those magazines. This was the late-70s when President Jimmy Carter was at the helm in the White House. The name of his National Security Advisor just stuck in my memory. So, when I mentioned the name of Zbigniew Brezinsky to my late friend Bill Estrem (a good American mentor and friend of mine who unfortunately passed away in February 2020) sometime in 2018 or 2019, he was surprised that I followed and remembered so much of American politics. The credit for all that should go to my father, who was my guiding light in broadening my vision, and therefore my horizons as well.

My Mathematics Coach – Helping Me Race from Zero to Hundred

Ironically, my ability to think critically came at a time when my performance in Mathematics reached its nadir in class VII. We had shifted to Ranchi in the summer of 1976, and mathematics was suddenly replete with lot of abstract concepts like rational numbers, polynomials, monomials, parallel lines, transversals, alternate angles, corresponding angles and the like. All this seemed Greek and Latin to a mind not yet given to critical and analytical thinking. And the result was something that ancient Indian mathematicians can take pride in contributing to the world of mathematics. The invention of zero. That was precisely my score in my first unit test.

I had no option but to break this terrible news to dad after he had returned from office. He was furious at what had become of my mathematical proficiency. There was a power cut that night at home. He lighted a candle, and taught me proper fractions, improper fractions, comparing fractions, and the like. That in hindsight was the beginning of my ability to think critically, analytically, and also learn to stretch my mental muscle.

After relocating to Hyderabad in the middle of our academic year in the winter of 1976, and managing to get admission into St. Anthony's High School through the good offices of our eldest maternal uncle, who was then Principal of Badruka College of Commerce in Hyderabad, and who knew the Principal of St. Anthony's High School, I and my sister managed to catch up on lost time and curriculum already covered. My challenges in Mathematics continued, albeit with a lot more improvement. I took tuitions from a Maths teacher, who sincerely taught me Mensuration (computation of area, volume, and total surface area) of two and three-dimensional objects. These sounded a lot more rational and understandable to my intellectual capacities at that point of time.

One challenge which I still wasn't able to get my head around was mathematical problems involving time and work. Problems like, "If 10 people can dig a trench 3 feet wide, 4 deep, and 10 feet length in 10 days, how long would it take 15 people to dig a trench 5 feet wide, 6 feet deep and 15 feet in length?" still continued to befuddle and confound me. My brother, who was brilliant in academics, employed a Q and A format to help me understand problems of time and work. He would break down the problem down to its smallest components, and pose questions on each component. Sometimes, I got it right, and sometimes I got it wrong. He would have a hearty laugh (after all, I was his kid brother), and he would endeavour to start all over again. I managed to get through my seventh grade, still befuddled by problems of time and work, and time and distance.

It was of course a different matter that in my eighth grade, Mathematics moved on to other mathematical concepts, leaving time and work, and time and distance behind. That was a partial relief, as the newer concepts presented in eighth grade posed different intellectual challenges, which I gamely tried to comprehend.

It wasn't until I reached ninth grade that I turned a little more studious, and with the help of my good friend Seshu (C.S.S. Sai), who gently nudged me to develop a love for mathematics by explaining to me mathematics with a little more depth, and a lot more patience than our average Math school teacher, my interest in mathematics started growing.

Nearly ten years later, as I was preparing to write competitive exams of banks, test of quantitative aptitude again brought back my old bogey of problems involving time and work. This time, I unabashedly approached my father, and he very lovingly taught me that the problems of time and work involved the fascinating interplay of fractions, and he ventured to explain me his assertion with a few problems involving time and work, and time and distance. What he taught me thirty-seven years ago is still fresh in memory, as his approach to teaching was based on logic and reason, and not mechanical problem solving as is the wont in teaching in schools.

In Class XI, in our quarterly exams, I scored 100% in mathematics. The one soul who was happier than me at my metamorphosis in mathematics was my father. The late blooming of my mathematical skills was to stand me in good stead as I ventured into a career in computing nearly a decade after this important milestone in my mathematical journey.

My First Cricket Coach

An important legacy that passed down from father to son was a deep and enduring love for cricket. Studying in a missionary school in Vijayawada in pre-Independent India brought my father in touch with two British influences that was unwittingly to stand my country in good stead in times to come. The first one was the English language that served to administratively unify a country of diverse languages and cultures. English was used as the medium of instruction, typically in missionary schools, which continues to this day. The second influence that captured the public imagination, and to which the people of India took to like a duck to water was the glorious game of cricket.

English missionary schools encouraged their wards to play cricket and hockey. Atkinson Senior Secondary School, where my father studied, was no exception. Though he played both cricket and hockey in school, cricket was his first love. I have heard him tell me that he used to play cricket with Anglo-Indian boys much senior to him. During the summer vacations, he would travel from his residence in Railway Colony, Vijayawada to Governorpet to play cricket matches. In one such match, a well-built Anglo-Indian fast bowler bowled a bouncer to dad. Dad didn't flinch, allowed the ball to come close to his nose, and then hooked the ball fearlessly for a boundary. The fast bowler, who was older to my dad, commended his courage and his technique in facing up to fast bowling.

After completing his schooling, my father shifted to Chennai to pursue his college education at Loyola College. Loyola College at that time had a very strong cricket team, which boasted of India hopefuls, A. G. Kripal Singh and A. G. Ram Singh. My father couldn't get into the First XI, but managed to play for the Second XI of Loyola College. Even after completing graduation, and joining A. G.'s Office, Chennai, he used to turn out for his office cricket team, and would play also for Mambalam Mosquitoes in the Chennai Cricket League. Even after moving to Hyderabad, and joining Electronics Corporation of India Ltd. as Company Secretary, he still found time to play for his office. On occasions, he even turned out for Reserve Bank of India's cricket team in Hyderabad's A Division Leagues, and would keep wickets. So here he was, a fearless batsman and a reliable wicketkeeper.

Dad Essaying a Backfoot Square Drive

And he would not miss Chennai's tryst with Test Cricket. Come Pongal time, the cricket itinerary of the Indian cricket team would include a test at the Chepauk stadium. Dad would be up early, buy tickets for the normal cricket stands, and his cousins and friends would join him later with lunch packed for all of them. And it was during these years that dad got to witness the genius of arguably the greatest ever cricketer, Sir Garfield Sobers. Arguably cricket's greatest allrounder, dad had seen him bat, bowl and field at the Chepauk. And the only phrases he used to describe Sobers' pure talent was feline grace and languid grace. Another cricketer from West Indies that he used to talk about was Rohan Kanhai, the dashing middle-order batsman. Dad had seen Kanhai essay his trademark falling hook shot. And as dad would recount to me the exploits of cricket's finest talents, my boyhood dreams also hoped to emulate these great cricketers.

The Long Room – Lords

In 1971, when I was six years old, my father initiated me into cricket. In our sparsely furnished middle class home in Ashok Nagar, Hyderabad, where the drawing room furniture consisted of three or four chrome-plated foldable chairs, the hall or the drawing room became the venue for my cricket initiation. He folded the chairs to create more space in the drawing room, and a very low wooden seat (referred to as Peetam in Tamil) was placed against the wall as stumps. Two parallel lines were drawn six inches apart, and he asked me to place my feet on those two lines. Just behind and slightly to the left of the line where my right foot was placed, he asked me to place the toe of the bat. He had got me a wooden bat for my age, so that I could wield the bat more easily. He moved over to the other end of the hall, and bowled to me with a rubber ball. My initiation into cricket had well and truly begun, and it must have happened at an auspicious time, for cricket became a lifelong love, and continues ever-strong at 59, a good 53 years and counting.

What I treasured most as a young boy of 6 or 7 were the used tennis balls he would get me from the ECIL Sports Club. After a few games of tennis, tennis balls go soft, and are rendered unusable in a tennis match. But they are good enough for a hit at short pitched cricket for boys my age then.

From rubber and tennis ball cricket, I quickly moved on to playing proper cricket with the big boys in our colony. Cricket balls were expensive, and could be bought from a sports shop at a royal sum of Rs. 7.50/-. This was the price of a cricket ball in the early and mid-seventies. But for middle class households, Rs. 7.50 was a significant amount of money. So, we would instead opt for the cheaper cork ball that came at around Rs. 2.00 or Rs. 2.50. But the problem with a cork ball was that it was much heavier compared to a cricket ball, and even the handle of a well-oiled cricket bat would come off if played with a cork ball.

And I played cricket with a cork ball without any protective gear. No leg guards, no gloves, and no abdomen protector. Helmets and chest guards were unheard of in cricketing circles in the timeline I am talking about. So, survival instincts took precedence especially when we went out to bat. We played barefoot, and getting a knock on the shins from a cork ball could be a very painful experience. So, I like most others, moved over to the leg side (not copybook cricket certainly), and then play our shots. It was one of cricket's dictums that to be a good cricketer, you must first overcome the fear of being hit by a cricket ball, or a cork ball. I for one couldn't get over this fear, and therefore, becoming a fine batsman was more or less ruled out.

My father on the contrary never feared being hit by a cricket ball even as he was approaching forty. An incident will bear this out. We were visiting our maternal uncle's place at State Bank Colony, Saidabad for a family function. It was a Sunday, and we all had gone down to attend the function. Dad was dressed in his traditional dhoti and a shirt. I joined my cousin (my namesake, but far more talented in cricket and far more illustrious than me) and his friends for a game of cricket. I just couldn't resist the pull of this game, wherever I happened to be. Very close to our uncle's house was an overhead water tank, and near it was a playground-like area good enough for a game of cricket. Behind the overhead water tank was the boundary wall of the colony, beyond which lay a thick wooded area.

On seeing us play, dad joined us for a brief hit with the bat. He folded his dhoti at the knee, and took strike. There was an Anglo-Indian friend of my cousin named Gordon who was an excellent cricketer, who excelled with both bat and ball. If I remember right, Gordon was getting ready to bowl, and my father was ready to take strike. Now, for a man approaching forty, and that too to bat in a dhoti wasn't the easiest thing to do. As Gordon ran in and pitched one in well up to the batsman, Dad took a stride down, got to the pitch of the ball, and lofted it straight over mid-on. It was such a big hit that it soared over the colony's boundary wall, and landed in the wooded area. My heart swelled with pride to see my cricketing hero play just one ball, but striking it clean. He then handed over the bat to us to continue our game. But that moment has remained etched in memory of my father's cricketing exploits.

My interest in cricket grew, and I started following the exploits of the Indian cricket team of the early-seventies. It was the era of radio, and I remember tuning into my uncle's newly acquired Philips radio to follow the ball-by-ball commentary of not only India's test matches, but also first-class cricket. I remember tuning into Radio Australia to follow the Australian team's exploits under the brilliant and inspiring leadership of Ian Chappell. Following the Indian team's tour to Australia meant getting up early to tune into the radio commentary. Dad watched me do all this, but never once discouraged me from playing and following the game. His gentle counsel to me was to show the same interest that I had in cricket (I would reel off cricket statistics from memory) to my academics as well.

My uncle was also a good cricketer, and used to turn out for his office team, his organization being the Reserve Bank of India. RBI had a good cricket team that regularly played the Hyderabad league, and on one such occasion, the RBI team played the Union Bank of India at the Welfare Cricket Ground, a large cricket ground that had a good turf wicket, had a good well-grassed outfield, and was just a five-minute walk from our home. These league matches would be played on Sundays, and I was one of the eager spectators who had gathered to watch the match. RBI had a strong cricket team, and RBI bowled first. RBI had a tall, lanky, bespectacled fast bowler named Vijayaraghavan. He bowled at a good pace and presented a straight seam, and his accurate and hostile bowling was more than a handful for the batsmen of Union Bank of India, who were bundled out for a small score. The RBI batsmen then knocked off the required runs in style.

After the match, uncle who knew Vijayaraghavan well, invited him home for a cup of coffee. And to my utter delight, Vijayaraghavan presented me with the ball with which he had bowled such a great spell. It was a treasure that landed in my hands, and I remember playing with the ball for a good amount of time.

The time must have been sometime in the year 1973. A few months ago, the English cricket team toured India for a five-test series under the captaincy of Tony Lewis. They had fine batsmen like Mike Denness, Dennis Amiss, Keith Fletcher, allrounder Tony Greig, a brilliant wicketkeeper and fine batsman Alan Knott, seam bowlers Geoff Arnold and Chris Old, and a quartet of spinners in Derek Underwood, Pat Pocock, Norman Gifford, and Jack Birkenshaw. There were other players who were part of the touring sixteen such as Graham Roope, Barry Wood, Bob Cottam, and Roger Tolchard.

Those were the days of radio commentary, and television was available in just a couple of cities in India, namely Delhi and Bombay (Mumbai now). Live telecast and match highlights therefore were unheard of. Fortunately, Films Division of India, that produced newsreels and documentaries, had compiled a two-hour capsule of the five test match series. It was being shown in Shanti theatre somewhere in Narayanguda in Hyderabad. Dad never liked movies, and he therefore rarely visited movie theatres. But once he came to know of Films Division airing the highlights of the test series, which he possibly got to know from the newspaper, he took me to the theatre, got the tickets, and there I was watching and enjoying the highlights to my heart's content. I was watching my cricketing heroes on celluloid for the first time. Memorable moments from the series included Vishwanath's century in the final test at Kanpur, and Tony Greig lifting little Vishy and holding him like a child, the exploits of the spin quartet that included Bedi, Prasanna, Chandra, and Venkat, and the amazing close-in catching of Eknath Solkar standing in the suicidal position of short leg with just an abdomen protector on. No helmets. No shin guards. Sheer guts and skill. This was an important milestone in my cricket education at the tender age of eight.

While in Class V, I tried getting into the junior school team (up to Class V) of my school, namely, All Saints High School. My school had a reputation for being one of the best school teams in cricket, and I couldn't manage to get selected into my school team. But that didn't deter my interest in cricket one bit. In fact, along with Dad, my school played an important role in furthering my cricket education. My school had produced champion cricketers who went on to play for State and Country, and notable among them being Syed Abid Ali, Sultan Saleem, Khalid Abdul Qayyum, Arshad Ayub, Mohammad Azharuddin, and Venkatapathy Raju. I was in Delhi in my second year in college, and when Azhar went on to score those three consecutive test hundreds on his debut test at Eden Gardens, Kolkata, and then scoring two more centuries in the next two tests at Chepauk, Chennai and Green Park, Kanpur, I was the tallest Hyderabadi walking the streets of Delhi.

Incidentally, in my second year in college, I first invested around 3-4 months to lose weight and get fit, and then joined the Bright Cricket Club in Delhi, which used to play in the B Division League in Delhi. During my brief stint with the club, I realized of my own accord that I had average cricketing talents, and there were team mates of mine who were far more talented than me. I did get to play a couple of friendly matches, but I had realized by then that cricket as a career was ruled out for me, as it required far more cricketing talent than what I had.

In 1986, Dad joined Indira Gandhi National Open University (IGNOU) as the founder Registrar. We shifted our accommodation from our humble MIG flat in Prasad Nagar to a five-level duplex style accommodation in Asian Games Village. In 1987, my father made his maiden visit to UK under a British Open University Exchange program. His visit was to study the best practices of the British Open University system, and incorporate some of those into IGNOU. His point of contact in Milton Keynes where British Open University was based was one Mr. Ted Jones. Incidentally, Mr. Ted Jones was a member of the MCC, and he took Dad on a tour of the Lord's Cricket stadium, considered by the cricketing community as the spiritual home of cricket. He even took Dad into the hallowed precincts of Lords, the Long Room, and the players dressing rooms. Dad had taken his Minolta SRT 101 camera, and he brought back lovely pictures of his visit to Lords, a necessary pilgrimage for every cricket lover. I was to follow in my father's footsteps in my maiden visit to the UK in the summer of 2008.

Coming back to my father's UK visit, he was given a shoestring allowance by his university. From that measly daily allowance, he saved enough to buy me a Gunn and Moore cricket bat for a royal sum of 50 GBP. It was a traditional cricket bat that needed to be oiled. He had played with a Gunn and Moore bat in his childhood days in Vijayawada, and he wanted me to have one. It was a nice light bat with perfect balance, well suited to my slight constitution. That is one of the most prized possessions which remains with me to this day. In fact, my mother sensing my generosity told me that the Gunn and Moore cricket bat that my father had got for me should be something that I should never give away to anyone. She didn't have to tell me that, but the fact that she gently told me so further reinforced my conviction to keep it as one of my most prized possessions, considering the love and sacrifice that went into my father buying it for me.

Now, I dwell on the most important part of the cricket education that my father imparted to me, which was the Spirit of Cricket. Cricket was always known as the gentleman's game upholding the highest standards of sportsmanship. The phrase "it's just not cricket", implying it is not fair is one of the key cornerstones of this great game. Cricket remains the only sport embodying the highest standards of fair play and sportsmanship. What my father taught me as part of my cricket education just didn't apply to the cricket matches I played, but was to shape my values and my world view as I grew into an adult.

Dad's Pilgrimage to the Spiritual Home of Cricket – Lords

As I recall my cricket of my boyhood days, what always stood out for me was enjoying a good game of cricket. Winning at all costs was never a priority. Winning and losing was part and parcel of playing a game of cricket, or for that matter, any other sport. And my love for this glorious game hasn't dimmed one bit, a good fifty-four years since that fateful day in 1971 when my father initiated me into cricket.

In conclusion, I will borrow the Great Bard's ode to Cleopatra's beauty to pay my rich tribute to this glorious game of cricket. "Age cannot wither her, nor custom stale her infinite variety".

Life Coach During My Adolescent Years

This is by far the most important and crucial role that my father played at a very important phase in my life. It's the twilight zone between childhood and adulthood; a time that is characterized by physical and emotional changes, and needs deft and skillful navigation. Before entering adolescence, I was this happy go lucky boy who was more engrossed with play, but managed to put in the minimum required hours of study to get above average grades in school.

Beginning Class IX, when adolescence had just about set in, I had in fact become a little more studious. And given whatever intellectual ability I had, I started taking more interest in studies. And with the help of my good friend Sai, the process of demystification of mathematics had well and truly begun. My Class IX academic performances were reasonably good, with History turning out to be my favourite subject. I underwent the same emotional and physical changes that Mother Nature mandates in the journey from boyhood to manhood. But in my case, these feelings were unsettling, and induced feelings of guilt, probably because of attraction to the opposite sex.

In Class X, the bogey of Board Exams was upon us, and I still managed my academics reasonably well, while the inner turmoil played on simultaneously. I was too shy to speak to anyone about this. For the Class X Board Exams, we had to study and prepare the combined syllabus of Class IX and Class X. Board Exams typically were scheduled in March, and our school gave us study leave for a better part of a month and a half. I fared reasonably well in my Board Exams, and then for the summer vacations, we came down to Hyderabad to spend time with our uncle and his family.

The Board Exam results were reasonably good, and I scored 67% in the Board Exams. As the schools reopened for the new academic season, it was time to choose our subjects for Class XI. What we choose now would go on to define our future course of study as we entered college to pursue our undergraduate program after completion of our school education. Since I felt that my fundamentals in Science, mainly Physics and Chemistry weren't too good, I choose the Commerce stream, all of my own volition. There was no pressure from dad to choose a particular stream.

New subjects, such as Accountancy, Commerce, and Economics, meant learning something anew. The pressure of learning new subjects, combined with below par teaching of these subjects, and my inner demons created a vicious cocktail that pulled me down in a downward spiral of below par scores in these new subjects. Ironically, it was during the quarterly exams in Class XI that I scored a perfect 100 in my mathematics. Even this bright spot couldn't paper over my less than satisfactory scores, particularly in Accountancy.

As an ordinary performance in Class XI transitioned into Class XII, the Board Exam bogey was once again upon us. Mathematics in Class XII ventured into the abstract such as three-dimensional geometry, and differential equations, which were proving difficult to comprehend and master. So, while good academic scores were a rarity to come by, my inner demons seemed to grow bigger by the day, exerting tremendous pressure on me. My young mind was overwhelmed by what was happening around me, and I slowly started giving in. Low self-confidence, little or no self-belief, and despondency took over my psyche, hurtling me toward what in retrospect I can now identify as depression.

Beginning the latter half of January, we were given preparation time for nearly a month and a half. So, while every student would make best use of this time to have a real shot at the Board Exams, I used to wake up every day with a blank mind, a sense of hopelessness, and utter despondency. And my inner demons of growing up characterized by recurring thought patterns, and guilt never let up in intensity. Unknowingly, I was fighting depression at a very young age.

Unable to bear all this, I finally bared my soul to my father. He lent me a compassionate ear, allowed me to make a clean breast of everything that had been troubling me, and then ventured to counsel me. His wise and sage counsel tried to calm me down saying that the problems of adolescence weren't new to me. He advised me not to fight or suppress my mind when faced with feelings of guilt. He was teaching me what The Buddha had taught when it came to managing one's mind. Just sit with your mind, and watch dispassionately whatever passes through it, pleasant, unpleasant or downright ugly. Just watch over these thoughts with awareness, while being aware of your breath, and these very obsessive thoughts cease to have any hold over you. My immature mind, while hearing out dad's counsel, was aspiring for the near impossible puritanical state. So, the very thing that you are trying to avoid seizes and takes hold of your mind. It is like the wise sage telling his disciple not to think about monkeys, and all that the disciple could think about was nothing but monkeys.

Another problem that my father sensed in his young son was the fear of exams, and wanting to run away in the heat of the battle. Fighting my inner demons, and my lack of self-belief and despondency had sapped me of all my mental energies. And this depression took such a hold on me that I was looking to clutch at every straw to avoid taking my exams. Here I was being caught in the classical Arjuna syndrome. A fine warrior who developed cold feet just at the onset of battle, as his own kith and kin stood against him in battle.

Lack of good preparations along with my mental distress convinced me that there was no point in me taking the exams. My father sensing this self-defeatist approach took a hardline, insisting that whatever be my level of preparations, I must face the exams. He didn't even accompany me to the exam centre to shore up my morale. He wanted me to face my own fears, fight my own battles, and emerge scarred but stronger in heart and spirit. At that time, I thought this was the most heartless decision a father could take regarding a son fighting his own battles. But in retrospect, it was one of the most important decisions that my father took in my eventual development into a strong and mature person, who developed the courage and the fortitude to face up to much sterner tests and battles, and emerge on the other side, wiser and stronger.

It was because of my father that I successfully completed my Class XII examinations with a reasonable score, without having to face the mortification of losing a year. But my struggles weren't to end so quickly. Depression can be a very dark place to be in, and it continued to play havoc with my graduation, as I was to discover shortly.

My two cents of wisdom on anyone suffering from depression is this. It can certainly be overcome by counseling sessions with a psychiatrist, and some medication. But in my case, I sought refuge in The Divine, and prayed for Providence to pull me out of this trough. And Providence did lend a helping hand to pull me out of the hole into which I had gotten myself into, but not before I was to endure more misery in the years to come during my graduation days. But the self-healing that I initiated on my own, though slow and tedious, was to make me mentally very tough in times to come.

Pulling Me Back From the Brink

Getting into a regular college for pursuing B.Com (Hons.) became difficult with my scores, and I therefore chose to pursue B.Com (Hons) from the School of Correspondence Courses and Continuing Education, University of Delhi. My late elder brother, who was then pursuing his Chartered Accountancy qualification, and who had a wise head on his shoulders, warned me against sitting at home and pursuing my B.Com (Hons) degree via Correspondence, saying I would never be able to discipline myself at home, and do the hard yards of regular study. But his wise counsel didn't register on my immature mind. But my father backed my decision, and I enrolled myself for a B.Com (Hons.) program at the School of Correspondence Courses and Continuing Education, University of Delhi.

As part of my study, I would keep in touch with two stalwart classmates of mine, Chandramauli, and Vasudeva Rao who were pursuing B.Com (Hons.) from Sriram College of Commerce, and Hindu College respectively. They would give me the prescribed texts for the various subjects, and I would buy those books, and do self-study on my own. But my brother's words turned prophetic. My love for cricket would get me distracted whenever Test Matches were telecast live on television. Almost the whole day would be spent watching the match. Dad had no objection to me watching cricket as long as I compensated for cricket time by getting up early, or sitting up late to finish my study designated for the day. But this hardly happened.

Low self-belief, low self-confidence and tons of self-doubt and despondency continued to dog me in my first year of college, and my scores in my first year of college were not good. In fact, they were a few notches below my Class XII score. The fallout of all this was that I became an introvert, and to ensure that I pursued my first love cricket with lots of zeal and energy, my father got me a complete cricket kit on my eighteenth birthday. But by then, I had put on weight, and my attention first turned to getting myself fit before venturing to seriously pursue cricket.

I went on a strict diet cutting out all my favourite fried stuff, and started jogging, which given my girth wasn't easy at all. I had to walk a couple of kilometers to the Salwan Public School grounds to do my jogging. And walk the two kilometers back home after my jog. And all this was undertaken in the hot summer months of June, July and August. By September, I had dropped considerable weight, and had become light on my feet. In October, I enrolled myself in Bright Cricket Club, which used to play in the Second Division League in Delhi. I was to discover very quickly that though I had a great love for, and had a good knowledge of the game, my talent was limited compared to my teammates, and this was a sobering realization that a career in cricket wasn't for me. But I continued playing in the limited opportunities I got. The initial months of January and February of the new year 1984 rolled by pretty quickly, and it was the first week of March.

Mom's paternal uncle had passed away in Hyderabad, and she wanted to be there for his death ceremonies, as her paternal uncles and aunts had taken on the responsibility of parents for her and her five siblings, and had conducted her marriage. I dropped my mother off at the New Delhi Railway Station in an auto, and to test my newfound reserves of stamina, decided to walk all the way home from the railway station. The weather was transitioning from winter to summer, and the warmth of the day coupled with the cool nights and cool early mornings isn't an easy environment for the body to adjust to. I came back home feeling normal, but by early next morning, I had a high fever. My father had to leave for office, and instructed my sister to take me to our family doctor. I was almost delirious with fever when my sister took me to the doctor. The doctor prescribed some fever-reducing drugs that I took on reaching home, but by late evening, I had developed red spots (purpura in medical parlance) on my body extremities. Our family doctor told my father that we should consult a specialist, and either the same night, or next morning, my father consulted Dr. A. N, Bhargava at Gangaram Hospital, and he immediately advised that I get admitted.

After admission, blood tests were done, and based on the blood test results that weren't too good, the doctor advised a bone marrow biopsy to be done. This development was unnerving to everyone. All the while, dad was with me at the hospital, while the home was in the care of my elder brother and sister. An SOS went out to my mother in Hyderabad about this test that was to be done next morning, and a flight ticket was booked for her to return the very same night. My brother received her at the airport, and brought her straight to the hospital. I don't really know the mental turmoil that she was going through, but she put up a brave front and told me not to worry, and that everything will be well.

The next morning, a doctor by the name Harsh Dua came to extract bone marrow from my lumbar region. Without any anesthetic, he injected a thick needle straight into my bone in the lumbar region for the bone marrow aspiration. The results were to be out in twenty-four hours. And during all these difficult hours, dad had taken leave from office, and was with me as my source of strength.

The next morning was a tense one for my family. I didn't even have the strength to feel any anxiety. So bad was my condition. The results came in around 9:00 or 10:00 am. To the utter relief of all concerned, the bone marrow test was negative. Dad's relief and joy knew no bounds. And in an immediate act of thanksgiving, he started reciting the Vishnusahasranamam. This was the first time that I was witnessing his firm and unshakable faith in The Divine. In the ebb and flow of life, the one thing that never changed, never dimmed, but remained a constant in his life was his faith in The Divine. I was to witness his resolute faith much later when tragedies came visiting our family.

In his professional life as well, though things did not go well for him, his dedication and commitment to his work never wavered even for a moment, and behind his strong mind and immense inner strength was his firm faith in The Almighty. He abided by Lord Krishna's counsel to do one's best, and not worry about the results. Since his professional life presents a fascinating study, I will dedicate a complete chapter to his professional life, and professional achievements.

Coming back to my illness, I was in hospital for a week after which I was discharged. I was a physical wreck when I came back home, and my mother tended to me like a baby to bring me back to good health. The journey back to good health was long and arduous, and I was faced with the immediate prospect of second year college exams, which were due in a couple of months.

My father being the persistent trier that he was asked me to prepare with whatever time I had, and take a shot at my exams. He never compelled me though, realizing my frail physical state, and left it to me to take a call. But given my history of less than mediocre results of the exams of the previous two years, I faltered in favour of skipping the exams that year. In retrospect, I feel that I should have heeded my father's counsel and given my best shot at the exams with whatever time and energy I had at my disposal. The loss of a year set me back psychologically in ways I never knew, and which I was to regretfully realize in the years to come.

Forbearance and Fortitude

My second-year exams got pushed back by a year, and when exam time came, I did write my exams, but not without the usual exam phobia, and inconsistent preparations that continued to haunt me. There were some papers that I cleared, and some I didn't, which got carried over to my next year. I again skipped the exams the ensuing year much to the chagrin and disappointment of my father. The year following that was marked by shabby preparations and taking the exams with predictable results.

I remember my father telling me clearly in one of our conversations that come what may, I had to complete my graduation. There just wasn't going to be any escape from this. As a parent, he realized that a basic graduation was the basic minimum on which further studies can be attempted, and a stable career can be built. It was at this time that I identified a good tutor, and dad backed this initiative of mine by allowing me to take tuitions from this tutor, who was a professor at Bhagat Singh college, and who used to stay at Kalkaji. I remember days bicycling to his residence from our residence in Asian Games Village, and going on to Outer Ring Road, and pedaling a good distance to reach his place. He was a good teacher who used humour to keep his students engaged, and ensure that the concepts hit home.

But apart from my tutor's help, there was no inspired or spirited effort in my preparations. It was patchy as before.

And as the summer months of 1988 rolled in, it was exam time. And this is where my father's implicit and unshakable faith in The Divine came to the fore. Even amidst his busy working schedule, he would fine time every Tuesday morning to make a visit to the Hanuman Temple in Jamuna Bazar near the ISBT terminus in North Delhi. Our residence was in South Delhi, and he would take time off to make the visit to the temple, which was easily twenty kilometers from our place, and return home in time to have a quick brunch and go to office.

Lord Hanuman was known to bless his devotees with courage, fortitude and intelligence. Sensing my diffidence, lack of self-confidence, and lack of self-belief, my father asked me to visit the Hanuman Temple in Jamuna Bazar. He had turned to his strong faith and was praying for Divine intervention to help his faltering son. I didn't refuse him, and agreed to visit the Hanuman temple. Amidst this doom and gloom, and my graduation lying in ruins, I still had a fair bit of rationality left in me. I wondered to myself, "How can God help someone who isn't willing to help himself?". With mixed feelings, I visited the Hanuman Temple at Jamuna Bazar as advised by my father.

My performance in my exams were comparatively marginally better than the previous failed attempts or no attempts, and judging by the percentage of questions that I attempted in the exams, getting over the line according to me was a near impossibility. As the month of July neared, it was time for my results to be out. Results of those enrolled with the School of Correspondence Courses and Continuing Education would come in a little later after the results of those enrolled with the regular colleges had been declared. With little or no hope, I went to check out my results. To my utter disbelief and pleasant shock, I had passed my exams; rather, I had scraped through. How I managed to do this is still a mystery to me, a good thirty-seven years after this had come to pass. The only one reason that I can fathom to explain this inexplicable happening is Divine Grace. The Divine out of sheer compassion not for me but for my father who kept his faith in Providence bailed out his lost son.

As I write these lines on a disastrous and immensely forgettable chapter in my academics, I now realize the immense amount of pain I would have caused my father. But he bore it all with courage and fortitude, willing to give his recalcitrant son opportunity after opportunity till his son somehow crossed the finish line with more than a nudge from The Divine, and infinite patience from him. I am close to completing sixty years shortly, and I have seen enough of human nature. And from my observation of life, I can confidently say that it is extremely rare to come across parents who stood by their son patiently and lovingly, doing everything they could for him, and waiting for him to cross an important academic milestone.

In retrospect, I now realize that I chose the wrong stream as I entered Class XI in my Senior Secondary years. That was the basic and fundamental reason of my not doing well during my college days. Again, it was up to my father to see my latent ability, and show me the right career to pursue that would help me put the bad memories of my college days behind me once and for all. More of that later.

A Reality Check

After completing my graduation, I evinced an interest to pursue Associate Company Secretaryship just like my father. I enrolled for the program, and started attending evening classes, which were conducted by practicing Company Secretaries. The subjects were interesting such as General Laws and Procedures, but what stood out conspicuously to dad was the lack of serious effort and study on my part in pursuing a professional qualification. Dad waited for a year, and then he decided that enough was enough, and it was time for his son to be given a taste of real life.

It was November 1989, and he took me to meet the Branch Manager of Godrej and Boyce for a suitable opening for me. All that they could offer me was the job of a Sales Canvasser, and I had to report into one of their senior marketing executives, one Mr. Dinesh Angirish. That was still the era of typewriters, manual and electronic, and I was given the Mayapuri industrial area to cover, and to sell typewriters. There was no monthly salary, but I was to be paid at the rate of Rs. 5/- per call, and I couldn't make more than ten calls a day. If any call resulted in the customer placing an order for a typewriter, I was to be paid some commission, the details of which I don't remember after all these years.

So, I would start off early from our home at Asian Games Village. First, I would take a bus to South Extension on Ring Road, and from there, I would take the Ring Road Service that would touch the periphery of Mayapuri on its way. I had no conveyance, and I had to walk into the industrial area from the Ring Road. I started right at the very beginning of Mayapuri, and would cover street after street in sequence. My mother would pack me a lunch, and I had no proper place to sit and eat my lunch. I would stand somewhere and eat my lunch, have a cup of tea at a roadside tea vendor, and would be off to cover my daily quota of ten sales calls.

I would do my work sincerely, and wouldn't just fill up the call sheets to fake sales calls that I had purportedly made. Sincerity and being truthful was a trait that I inherited from my parents. I worked as a sales canvasser for close to three months. I never fancied myself as a fine communicator, which is an essential skill for a salesperson, but in spite of this constraint, my sincerity fetched Godrej orders for six typewriters from six different clients.

It was during my forays into Mayapuri industrial area that I came in close contact with the harsh realities of life. Workers working in the factories here worked in unsafe conditions, and it was the sheer compulsion of earning a livelihood that made these workers compromise their safety, and work in extremely unsafe conditions for their wages, which would put food on the table for their families. This was the education that my father wanted me to have, which couldn't be taught in the comfort of a home.

Spotting My Latent Analytical Ability

In the situation I was in, the best thing for someone would have been to remove oneself from everything, and see oneself from a distance to get an objective perspective of what could potentially be one's areas of strength, and the best way to tap into these. At that point of time, I didn't have the emotional and intellectual maturity to embark on this exercise.

My father again stepped in to help me out of this difficult situation. Just like a sports coach spots a rare talent after watching a sportsperson briefly, and then giving him/her a roadmap to follow to realize his/her talent and potential to the full, my father spotted something in me to which I was oblivious to all along. In a multidisciplinary sport like cricket, there have been cricketers who started off as top order batsmen, but then on the advice of the coach have gone on to don a different role such as an off-spinner and leave a lasting impact on the game. I am talking of Ravichandran Ashwin, who on the advice of his coach switched from being a top order batsman to spin bowling. Another shining example of this is one of India's premier batsmen, Rohit Sharma, who started off as a youngster bowling spin, but the razor-sharp eye of his coach saw tremendous potential in Rohit Sharma as a batsman, and asked him to instead focus on batting, and the rest as they say is history.

All through the one year after completing my graduation, my father's constant refrain to me was to do a Diploma program in Information Technology. The Information Technology industry was just starting to take off, and my father had the foresight to realize that this was a sunrise industry, and was likely to grow tremendously in the years to come. My father was the first one to spot my latent analytical ability, and realized that I wasn't cut out for pursuing ACS that I had enrolled for.

Even as I was doing my sales canvasser job for Godrej, he kept persuading me to do a Diploma Program in Information Technology. I enquired from NIIT, India's premier IT training institute then, regarding the courses on offer. They were offering a three-semester, eighteen-month Post Graduate Honours Diploma program in Systems Management that cost ten to twelve thousand rupees. That was a lot of money in 1990. And my fear was that after my father paying such a big sum for my post graduate computer diploma, I shouldn't botch it up like my graduation, and let my father down. When I voiced these apprehensions to my father, he said something that would have lifted the spirits of someone who was down and out. He said, "Son, just go ahead and do this course. Even if it weren't to turn out to our expectations, I would consider it money well spent". When I heard my father say this, a great burden lifted off my shoulders.

But one condition that my father put was that I must continue working as a sales canvasser during the day, and attend my computer classes in the evening (my class timings were 5:30 – 7:30 p.m.). For a couple of weeks, I tried working and attending classes, but there were a couple of occasions when I had difficulty getting a public transport bus, and reaching my class on time. I then expressed my desire to my father to devote myself full-time to my computer course, and a father's wisdom by then had realized that his son had learnt his lessons well and he relented.

I took to computing like a duck to water. The first two tests on flowcharting and COBOL programming secured me a 100%. COBOL being a structured programming language, with its emphasis on top-down coding, was something that resonated with my own bent of reasoning and problem solving. Semester I passed off like a breeze with my grades being very good. Semester II exposed us to microdatabases, spreadsheets, and Structured Systems Analysis and Design, propounded by the pioneering duo of Edward Yourdon and Tom DeMarco. Much later in my professional life, while working for Wipro Technologies, I was nominated by my organization to attend the Cutter Consortium in Boston, Massachusetts in May 2007, and it was a privilege and an honour to hear these two gentlemen speak at the consortium.

I managed microdatabases well, but spreadsheets were slightly tricky. And I was again faced with comprehending abstract concepts when we moved on to understanding Systems Analysis and Design. But I was persistent in my efforts to get to the bottom of it, and in course of time, with more exposure and reading of the subject, and allowing it a significant portion of my mindshare, the subject unraveled itself. Second semester scores weren't as good as semester I but still good enough. And the most challenging of all for me at that time given my intellectual maturity then was UNIX and C programming. But I soldiered on with a classmate, Raghuraj Hulkar, who became a good friend of mine, and who helped me in understanding a tricky concept like Recursion. During our third semester, the Mandal Commission agitation broke out all over India, and Delhi was no exception. This agitation was championed by the student community against unwarranted increases in reservation for the underprivileged (what we refer to as affirmative action in the West), and classes got disrupted, including ours at NIIT. My course, which should ideally have gotten over by June 1990, stretched by an additional 6 months.

After the completion of my third semester with a reasonably good score, I was finally awarded the Diploma of Post Graduate (Hons.) Diploma in Systems Management from NIIT. My father's gamble had paid off big time. The punt that he had taken on an errant son had reaped rich dividends. It was now time for the Placement Cell at NIIT to get me a suitable opening in the nascent IT industry. More of that in the next chapter.

A Career in IT – A Dream Come True

I must make a specific mention of my third semester faculty, one Ms. Lubna Afaque, who not only taught us a part of semester III, but was also heading the placement cell of my NIIT center. She put in a lot of sincere effort in securing for me two openings, one at Indian Market Research Bureau, and Hindustan Office Products Ltd. (HOPE Ltd.). As per the placement terms, I had to take the first offer that was made to me. I preferred joining IMRB, but unfortunately, the offer letter from HOPE Ltd. came in first, and I had to take the offer.

I joined HOPE on 11th February 1992, as an Associate Applications Analyst. The challenge for me was that nothing of what I had learnt in my computing course came handy in my first job. I was recruited to develop applications for a Palmtop (a handheld computing device) that had its own proprietary Operating System, and its own proprietary programming language. I therefore had to scramble, and learn the new operating system and programming language at the earliest. My senior, who was more experienced and knowledgeable than me, would never help me in getting up to speed, possibly out of his own sense of insecurities. I therefore had to learn on my own, albeit using the trial-and-error approach, and I realized early on that you are your own best teacher. Expecting a colleague to help you out in a world of cutthroat competition was being utterly naïve.

HOPE Ltd. had quality issues with their hardware. Their storage media called data packs would size because of power not being stable on the Palmtop device and causing data loss, and therefore one fine day, the Board of Directors took the extraordinary decision of changing character from a manufacturing company to a trading company. The first exercise undertaken when such major restructuring of an organization happens is layoffs. Between me and my senior, my organization naturally preferred my senior, and my manager called me in early September 1992 to tell me that my services weren't required, and that I can start looking out for a new job. He had the grace to tell me that I needn't attend office, but could use my time to look out for suitable openings.

This hit me really hard. Within seven months of my first job, I was being fired. And a layoff can really dent your confidence. I broke the news to my father, who consoled me saying this is all a part and parcel of a career, and that I mustn't lose hope, and instead redouble my efforts at finding myself a suitable opening. In the early nineties, UNIX, RDBMS and C were the most sought-after skills in the IT industry. And I reasoned that one of the best ways to master a subject is to first learn it thoroughly and then teach it.

I then took the important decision to return to my Alma Mater, not as a student, but as a Faculty. I went through a rigorous recruitment process, and multiple rounds of interviews. At one stage, I had all but given up. But then came the call for the final interview, and the Centre Head Mr. Varun Khanna of the NIIT Centre at South Extension, where I was to eventually join interviewed me. I fared reasonably well, and then I had one more interview, just to put a touch of finality to my recruitment. My Regional Manager, Mr. Rajiv Katyal interviewed me, and I was in. I joined NIIT as a faculty on 20th November 1992. I learnt the ropes of being an effective faculty from helpful colleagues (lot of them to mention here). NIIT South Extension had in fact, two centres, one right on the ring road, and the other a smaller centre, right behind the one on the main road. I was recruited to teach in the smaller centre, and its new center head who kind of joined along with me was one Mr. Apurva Sharma.

Under the able guidance of my colleagues, and my two centre heads, my career as a faculty gradually took wings. I shed the inhibitions that being an introvert generally brings, and started communicating more. And effective communication is the most effective tool in the hands of a teacher to convey his/her subject to his/her students. I attended a few training programs in communication skills and student management.

Around the summer of 1993, summer programs would be conducted in BASIC for school students. One of my colleagues who was taking one such program had a unique exercise given. The exercise was on the number 1729. A few months prior to this, I had bought and read the biography of India's finest mathematician, Srinivasa Ramanujan, written beautifully by Robert Kanigel. The story of Ramanujan is indeed fascinating, for he was entirely self-taught, and he sent his mathematical papers to the British mathematician G. H. Hardy, who immediately spotted his genius, and called him over to England. Ramanujan and Hardy were to collaborate and publish a lot of papers. But due to Ramanujan's orthodox upbringing, and his strict adherence to vegetarianism, he contacted TB and was in hospital in England receiving treatment. Hardy would make a visit daily to call on Ramanujan at the hospital, and in one of these visits, he remarked to Ramanujan that the cab number 1729 of the cab that he took to reach the hospital was very uninteresting. To which Ramanujan immediately exclaimed to Hardy, "Don't say that. It's a beautiful number. It's the least positive integer expressible as the sum of the cubes of two numbers in two different ways ($9^3 + 10^3$, and

$12^3 + 1^3$). I distinctly remembered this interaction between the two mathematical geniuses in the book, and when problem of 1729 presented itself to one of my colleagues, I gave them the answer as elucidated above.

My Centre Head, Apurva Sharma was looking over my shoulder as I was giving my colleague the solution to the problem of the number 1729. Though I was only 27 at that time, I had greyed a lot, and coupled with my droopy moustache, and a general disposition of being lost in my own world, he gave me a nickname that soon spread to other centres as well. He gave me the name Einstein. I do confess that Albert Einstein is my idol, and liked the nickname Einstein, but I wasn't even a patch on arguably the greatest physicist of the 20th century.

It was during this time in NIIT that I was mentored by my Center Head, Mr. Varun Khanna. Seeing my affinity for programming, he advised me to widen my reading and suggested that I read the book, "Godel, Escher, Bach: An Eternal Golden Braid" by Douglas Hofstadter. This book drew on the common themes of three brilliant individuals in their respective fields, Kurt Godel in Mathematics, the mathematical drawings of M. C. Escher, and the musical works of Johann Sebastian Bach. One of the common themes picked up and elaborated by the author in the works of these three luminaries was recursion. Here was a concept in programming resonating with Mathematics, Music, and Drawing. This was revealing and an eye opener for me. I realized how seemingly unrelated subjects could have a convergence, and reading this book had a significant impact in my intellectual development, and in broadening my vistas of understanding.

Varun also once talked to me of the Pygmallion Effect. This is a concept in psychology wherein if you set someone a higher benchmark, he strives to achieve that benchmark, either meeting it, or just about falling short of it, but in the process exceeding his abilities. Varun wanted me to use the Pygmallion Effect with my students, setting them higher benchmarks, and motivating and guiding them to better themselves. Without saying so, Varun was actually indirectly telling me to better myself, and eventually to exceed my own abilities.

The reason for this digression has a specific reason. In both the aforesaid events, I have drawn on my extra reading that eventually broadened my perspective, and made me think unconventionally in trying to understand a difficult concept, and use innovative and simple methods to convey the same to my audience. And the credit for this habit of extra reading should again go to my father, who had inculcated this reading habit in my boyhood days a long time ago. The reading habit doesn't develop overnight, and here was dad's foresight paying off in rich measure.

In the same summer of 1993, I and another colleague of mine Thanigai were nominated to attend a training on Computer Networking that was making waves around that time. The world was moving on from standalone computers to networks. The specific network operating system that we got training on was Novel Netware, by far the leading network operating system then. After undergoing training, our centre head gave both of us the responsibility of networking the computers in our computer lab. The entire concept and execution was done by my good friend Thanigai, with I solely playing the role of assisting him. We sat in office the whole night, and our deadline was to finish the installation by 7:00 am the next morning, for the first morning batches would come in by 7:00 am. Here was a wonderful colleague and an enduring friend who shared all his knowledge and expertise with me, unlike my senior in my first job.

But the tenure at NIIT was a bitter-sweet one, and I decided to separate from the organization after three-and-a-half years of dedicated work, often exceeding my call of duty. But the rewards for my commitment just weren't there. After I was passed over for a promotion for two consecutive years, I decided that I had become a liability to the organization, and didn't want to live on the organization's charity. I was so hurt by my appraisal letter that I broke down in office (one of the very rare occasions I had broken down in public), and decided then and there that I will resign forthwith from the organization.

My emotional decision to quit had a different response from my elder brother and dad. My elder brother's counsel was more grounded and pragmatic, saying I should continue working, while at the same time looking out for openings. On the other hand, my father understood the mental agony of his son for not getting recognition at the workplace (my father was an outstanding professional who was my idol, and yet he endured disappointments at the workplace not because of anything lacking from him, but buy the treatment that was meted out to him by his superiors), and he okayed my decision to call time.

The next day, I went to office, and applied for long leave. I don't remember taking even a day's leave in my stint at NIIT, and I used this much-deserved leave to upgrade myself in RDBMS skills (Oracle) and its front-end tool then, Developer 2000. This was the Client-Server era, and Developer 2000 jostled for programmer mindshare as a leading client-end development tool along with other popular tools such as PowerBuilder, Visual Basic, and SQL Windows. I underwent training at SQL Star Ltd., which was an Oracle-authorized training partner. The Delhi Branch Manager was quick to spot from my enrollment form that I was a faculty at NIIT, and after completing my course, he interviewed me. A little time later, the then DGM of SQL's Education Division, Mr. Ramlal who was visiting Delhi interviewed me, and my appointment as a faculty at SQL Star Ltd. was finalized. Mr. Ramlal later went on to become the Vice President of the Education Division, and became my mentor, guiding me to become a more evolved version of myself as a technology trainer.

Here again, the point I would like to emphasize is the critical role played by my father in ensuring a smooth transition from one organization to another. I went on to work in SQL for seven years, in the course of which I widened my repertoire of skills, and more important, my work got due recognition at SQL. I chose to part with SQL only after waiting a couple of years when the organization had started going downhill in the aftermath of the dotcom bust in 2000, and only when I was reasonably sure that I was risking my career and my future there, I chose to move on and join Wipro Technologies.

I worked in Wipro for close to eight years, and my final stop in my career journey was Tata Consultancy Services. A month before joining TCS was a time of emotional tumult in the family, with my elder brother passing away in Delhi due to renal failure that he battled bravely for eight years. After completing my brother's ceremonies, I had just under three weeks to emotionally recover, and be ready to join TCS. Before joining TCS, I remember having an interesting conversation with my father, wherein I told him that TCS will be my last stop in my career journey. I remember telling him that I will work in TCS for as long as I can, and I won't precipitate my resignation, but the day I chose to leave TCS would be the day I would call time on my career.

That day did transpire after close to five years at TCS. After nearly three-and-a-half years of a fruitful tenure at TCS, there were a lot of changes within the organization. My supervisor Mr. Vidyut Navalkar, who was a thorough gentleman was asked to find himself another role within the organization. A new VP was thrust upon us, who did not understand a whit of the training function, and was given to talking out of his hat. The dilemma facing me was to endure his inanities, forsaking my professional integrity, or choose the honourable way out by exiting the organization. I chose the latter option, and on 13th December 2015, I called time on my twenty-five-year career in the IT industry. In hindsight, it was a decision I haven't regretted even nine years after taking the decision. From a personal standpoint, I felt it was my duty as a son to give my ageing parents more time, which I wasn't able to during the course of my busy career.

And in conclusion, my checkered career in the IT industry wouldn't have come to pass but for my father's infinite patience, his faith in me that I would turn the corner one day, seeing my potential for computing, and backing it to the hilt. So, my entire career is dedicated to my father as a tribute to him.

A Beacon of Consistent Professional Excellence

This is by far the most fascinating chapter of this book. I will trace his life from his school days to college days, and from there to his career taking shape in a most fascinating and inspiring manner. Much of what is going to unfold here is based on my father's own account of his childhood days, attending school and college, and finally his career taking off. Some of the details of his college days have been added in by my uncle, as my father, given his modest demeanour, never spoke of his own accomplishments.

His Professional Mentor – My Maternal Granduncle

It's a setback to a child at age nine to lose a father. And that is precisely what happened to dad. In 1943, when dad was nine years old, my grandfather passed away, leaving the family of five siblings (four brothers and a sister) to be managed by my grandmother, a brave and intrepid woman. She was a woman endowed with practical wisdom, could read and write her mother tongue Tamil, and keep accounts of household expenses. But in matters of providing guidance and direction to her sons still in early stages of their education, she was hamstrung, as she didn't have the benefit of a formal education.

Birds of a Feather Flock Together

This is where the importance of understanding the value of a formal education dawned pretty early on dad. My grandfather had put him in a missionary school in Vijayawada, and dad completed his formal schooling there, and it was now time to pursue junior college or intermediate studies. Dad realized that Vijayawada didn't have colleges of standing where he could pursue his higher education, and he therefore impressed upon my grandmother to have their home in Chennai vacated and readied for them to move in, so that they could all stay in Chennai, making it easier for all the other siblings also to pursue their studies.

With his Professional Idol J. R. D. Tata, who was visiting the ECIL Campus

He joined Loyola College, Chennai, a college known for all-round excellence. He pursued Mathematics and Physics in his intermediate studies, and excelled in both, a fact little known in family circles. The natural extension when it was time to pursue his graduation was to pursue a graduate program in Physics, which he applied for. To be on the safe side, he also applied for a graduate program in B.Com. The rule prevalent in Madras University then was that whichever course put out its admission list first is what you have to take, and moreover dad got a scholarship from Loyola College, on grounds of having lost his father early. Dad had no option but to pay the reduced fee and enroll for B.Com, as the B.Com list came out first. Within a day or two, the B.Sc. (Physics) that he had applied for also released its admission list, and dad's name figured there as well. Unfortunately, he had to let go of his ambition to pursue Physics. If that had materialized, who knows, he might have gone on to excel himself as a Physicist of great standing.

With Colleagues; Specific Mention of Guruswamy uncle and uncle Devgaonkar, to the Left of Dad

Undeterred by this small setback, he pursued B.com with great commitment, and stood seventh in the University upon the completion of his B.Com. His graduation completed in 1954, a fact corroborated by my uncle, and very shortly that same year, he joined Accountant General's Office in Chennai as an Upper Division Clerk. In mid-1955, he got married to my mother in Hyderabad, and after marriage, as is the custom, my mother moved to Chennai along with my father to be part of a large household that was being managed by my grandmother.

But dad wasn't content with the job of a UDC in AG's Office. He had a burning desire to further his education, and better his career prospects. The next logical step was to pursue a degree in law (LLB). But there was a problem. Madras University did not offer an evening college option for pursuing a degree in law. They only offered a day college option. It was at this juncture that my mother's paternal uncle (who was almost a father to her as he took care of her and conducted her marriage after the passing away of my maternal grandfather) stepped in and became a father figure to dad. He was working in a private company in Hyderabad, and he told dad that Osmania University in Hyderabad offered an evening college option for pursuing a degree in law, and if dad wished to pursue law, he could come down to Hyderabad, and he would use his good offices in the private company where he worked to secure a commensurate employment for dad there.

The August Board of ECIL, including Dr. Homi N Sethna, Dr. Vikram Sarabhai, and Dr. A. S. Rao

It was at this critical juncture that dad took one of the most courageous decisions in his life. He took the decision of giving up the comforts of a government job, which was, and is still very much sought after, as it offered job security. In the late-fifties, resigning from a government job was tantamount to sacrilege, but my father still went ahead and resigned from AG's Office after putting in more than four years of service there. There was a lot of opposition from his family elders, particularly his maternal uncles, who felt it was foolhardy on dad's part to resign from a government job, and instead opt for employment in a private company.

The August Board of ECIL, including Dr. Raja Ramanna, Dr. N. B. Prasad, Dr. Homi N. Sethna. Dad at extreme left.

In 1959, he moved to Hyderabad along with my mother and my elder brother, who was under two years old then. He joined the private company where my granduncle worked, and started pursuing his law program in the evening college offered by Osmania University. And private companies then and even now have a reputation for squeezing their employees hard. My father was no exception to this truism, and he had to log in long hard hours of work, manage his family, financially support my grandmother in Chennai, and still find the energy to study and clear his law exams. Which he did successfully.

The next qualification that he aimed for was to become an Associate Company Secretary (ACS), a corporate professional program launched by the Institute of Company Secretaries of India (ICSI), which had just been set up. My granduncle was one of the first to pursue and acquire this qualification, and dad inspired by his father figure now, enrolled himself for the ACS program. And by the summer of 1965, he had successfully completed the ACS program. After completing the ACS program, ICSI mandated that successfully qualified candidates had to undergo professional training. Dad chose to undergo professional training at Addison Co. Ltd. in Chennai. He was undergoing the training in Chennai when I was born. Both my youngest paternal and maternal uncles provided the moral and material support to my mother, along with my mother's aunt, who would invariably come down to attend to mother and child.

With Dr. Manmohan Singh at IGNOU campus, then Chairman UGC, and later to don the role of Finance Minister, and Prime Minister of India

After returning from his training, dad set his sights higher. He applied for the post of Deputy Company Secretary at Hindustan Aeronautics Limited, Bangalore and got selected. In 1966, dad, mom, my elder sister and I (just one year old) moved to Bangalore, with my elder brother staying on in Hyderabad with my maternal aunt to pursue his schooling.

With Dr. Manmohan Singh at IGNOU campus, then Chairman UGC, and later to don the role of Finance Minister, and Prime Minister of India

As per the Companies Act, 1956 which was applicable then, it was the responsibility of the Company Secretary to first of all create an agenda for the Board meeting, and circulate it to all Directors on the Board. The Company Secretary under whom my father worked was a retired Squadron Leader from the Indian Air Force, who after retiring joined HAL as Company Secretary. It was, and is still the practice of the Government of India to accommodate retired armed forces personnel at suitable positions in Public Sector Undertakings (PSU), and Hindustan Aeronautics Limited was a PSU. After successfully conducting the Board Meeting, it was the responsibility of the Company Secretary to record the Minutes of the Board meeting in a register, which is under the custody of the Company Secretary. And the convention then was to record the Minutes of the Board meeting in neat handwriting

Seeing off Dr. Manmohan Singh after a memorable visit to the IGNOU campus

This Company Secretary, who was coopted from the Air Force saw my father's excellent drafting skills, and his wonderful handwriting. But to make it appear as if recording of the Minutes of the Board meeting was done by him, he would ask Dad to type out the Minutes of the Board meeting, and would affix his signature. Such was the insidious attempt made by this Squadron Leader turned Company Secretary (God alone knows how much of Company Law or General Laws he knew), who wished to suppress the talents of his Deputy Company Secretary. This was something my father shared with my mother, and my mother in turn related this incident to me to show how my father's talents and capabilities were sought to be suppressed.

I don't know the timelines now, but I distinctly remember dad telling me that he cleared Civil Services – Preliminaries as well as Civil Services – Mains. What proved to be a stumbling block was the interview, which he couldn't crack. In a candid moment, he shared with me that he lacked confidence, especially when giving the interview for Civil Services, and wished he had his father by his side.

With the Then Commonwealth Secretary General – Mr. Sridath Ramphal

On April 11, 1967, the Electronics Corporation of India Limited was established in Hyderabad under the stewardship of Dr. A. S. Rao, the first Managing Director of this Public Sector Undertaking. Dad saw this opening, and immediately applied for the post of Company Secretary. He was interviewed and selected as ECIL's first Company Secretary. There was no Department of Electronics then, and ECIL was put under the purview of the Department of Atomic Energy. There were many stalwarts in the Department of Atomic Energy, and three brilliant minds from the Department of Atomic Energy who were on the Board of ECIL were Dr. Homi N Sethna, Dr. Vikram Sarabhai and Dr. Raja Ramanna. One more Board member was Dr. N. B. Prasad, who was Chairman of Oil and Natural Gas Commission (ONGC). My father had the good fortune to be in such august company. As a young boy of 8 or 9, I remember dad telling me about these individuals of high standing, who were all brilliant minds working for the country. With their qualifications, they could have easily gone on to work in Europe or America, and made lots of money, but this was a generation of men who were committed to nation building.

The First Convocation of IGNOU, With the Then Prime Minister Rajiv Gandhi Presiding Over the Function

My father acquitted himself very well in his role as Company Secretary, and is the case with honest and diligent employees, he was saddled with the added responsibility of Administration, which at the best of times, is a thankless job. The office canteen and office transport came under Administration, and I remember my father keeping tabs and conducting surprise inspections to check and curb malpractices in the canteen and transport. This took a lot of his time and energy. He had also enrolled himself for the Cost Accountancy program under the aegis of the Institute of Cost Accountants of India. He was just left with a single group in his CWA final which he unfortunately couldn't complete, having completed his intermediate, and the remaining groups in his CWA final. Had he stuck to just his role of a Company Secretary, he would certainly have been a qualified Cost Accountant as well.

The Convocation Protocol – The University Registrar Leading the Other Leading Functionaries of the University

During his tenure in ECIL, which was from 1967-1975, he mentored many under him. In 1975, he moved on from ECIL to Hydrocarbons India Ltd., a wholly-owned subsidiary of ONGC. Dad was given a grand farewell at ECIL, and many of his colleagues, including those he mentored came to see him off at the railway station. Prior to his farewell, he had joined Hydrocarbons India Limited in early 1975, and had spent a couple of months at his dear friend, uncle Devgaonkar's house in Delhi. Uncle was Dad's colleague at ECIL, and they were close friends. Uncle had moved on from ECIL to Central Electronics Limited in Delhi much before Dad. He had shifted with his family (aunty and two daughters) to Delhi barring his son Subodh who was to be my classmate in our school days in Delhi, and continues to be a good friend even now. I, mom, and my sister along with Subodh were traveling with dad to Delhi by the Dakshin Express, which would entrain from Nampally at 8:50 pm. I was a boy of ten. But even after a good fifty years, the memories of that day are still fresh. A couple of his colleagues that he mentored broke down and wept at the station. Grown up men crying was something I was seeing for the first time. As I reflect on that incident now, I realize how much my father meant to them in terms of mentoring them, guiding them, and providing them a roadmap for their career. He made men of them.

The Convocation Protocol – The University Registrar Leading the Other Leading Functionaries of the University

In his condolence message to me, uncle Devgaonkar mentioned dad as his friend, philosopher and guide. Dad used to affectionately call him Dev, and theirs was a friendship worth emulating. Both of them succeeded in forging a strong familial bond between their respective families, and after we moved to Delhi, reciprocal visits on weekends were a given. They would relish mother's wonderful south Indian preparations, and we would in turn delight in the Maharashtrian cuisine that aunty would prepare for us (pitla-bakri, Pooran poli, and zunka-bakri to name a few).

The Registrar Addressing the Convocation

I would henceforth refer to his tenure at Hydrocarbons India Limited as tenure at ONGC. During his tenure at ONGC as Company Secretary, he got the opportunity to go abroad on official work. ONGC had tie-ups with an Iranian oil company, and also AGIP of Italy. During his tenure at ONGC, he made multiple trips to Tehran and also Milan. He would invariably return from his visits to Tehran with lots of dry fruits, and they were pretty cheap then, since they were available in plenty. This was the Iran of the pre-revolution days under the Shah of Iran, Shah Mohamad Reza Pahlavi. As part of his official schedule, dad once took a helicopter from Tehran to Lawan island to see a major oil rig that Iran has on that island.

Bridge between the Past and the Present – The Registrar with the current and previous Vice Chancellors of IGNOU, Dr. V. C. Kuzhaindaswamy and Prof. G. Ram Reddy

Though Milan is referred to as the fashion capital of the world, Dad never had that kind of allowances to buy clothes of expensive labels. But I remember him getting us tee-shirts in one of his visits, a Moulinex mixer, a Moka percolator, and a Termozeta iron for ironing our clothes. These were simple joys of a grounded middle-class family. He even got me a pair of roller skates from Milan. It is still in my possession, a good fifty years after.

But his joy in ONGC was short-lived. Dad became collateral damage in the board-level politics between the Managing Director and Director Finance. For dad to survive in such a vitiated atmosphere would have meant going against his grain of being noble, straightforward and truthful. Rather than use cunning to survive that would have been the only way out, he valued his integrity more, and put in his papers at ONGC, but not before securing for himself the post of Company Secretary at Central Mine Planning and Design Institute (CMPDI), a wholly-owned subsidiary of Coal India Ltd.

Dad Speaking at His Superannuation Function at IGNOU – 30th June 1994

This required us to move to Ranchi, which was part of the state of Bihar then, and is now capital of the newly carved out state Jharkhand. Unwittingly, we had stepped into the Wild East, figuratively speaking. Dad's colleagues at CMPDI warned him against transferring his Provident Fund from ONGC to CMPDI, for they said that it would become part of the Coal Miners Provident Fund, which was controlled by the coal mafia there, and it would be very difficult for dad to get that money out. Moreover, Patna University then was notorious for exam backlogs, and we had stepped into a state where the standard of Hindi in our schools was high for I and my sister to keep up to. Sensing our academic dilemma, dad did something that only a loving and devoted father would do.

Dad Being Felicitated at His Superannuation

He decided to rejoin ECIL, not as Company Secretary, as his Deputy, Mr. G. S. R. Murthy, who was also a good family friend, had been elevated to the post of Company Secretary after Dad moved out of ECIL. He decided to rejoin as Manager – Administration; a decision that he wasn't comfortable with, but took it in the long-term interests of his children and his family. We joined St. Anthony's High School, Himayat Nagar, Hyderabad in the middle of the academic season in November 1976. My eldest Mamaji, who was Principal of Badruka College of Commerce, knew the Principal of St. Anthony's High School very well, and it was Mamaji interceding on our behalf, which was instrumental in the school admitting us. The Principal of St. Anthony's High School had his pound of flesh though, asking for a donation of Rs. 350/- each for me and my sister. That was a significant amount of money in 1976, and my father paid the donation and the fees, and both I and my sister were on our way.

Both I and my sister acquitted ourselves well in Class VII and Class IX exams respectively. But dad wasn't professionally happy, and within a year of having rejoined ECIL, he resigned and joined Electronics Trade and Technology Development Corporation (initially known as ETTDC, and later as ET & T, but nowhere near in capability to its similar-sounding American counterpart). We moved back to Delhi in the summer of 1978, and I and my sister resumed our schooling in the same school where we had studied earlier in the 1975-76 academic year, D. T. E. A. Senior Secondary School, Mandir Marg.

CEMCA and IIMC Collaborating on the Educational Applications of Multimedia. Seated Fourth from Left is Dr. Sugata Mitra, Pioneer in Education, and Who Envisioned the Hole-in-the-Wall Experiment that stimulated Autonomous Learning in Children

In the third week of January 1981, after attending our cousins' wedding in Hyderabad, we returned back to Delhi in time for dad to attend what was eventually a very ill-fated Board meeting. The Chairman and Managing Director (CMD) and the Director Finance were at daggers drawn, and in that meeting, the Director Finance cleverly maneuvered to remove the CMD. The Director Finance perceived my dad to be close to the CMD, and what ensued for the next one year was utter mental torture for dad. The Director Finance held out a threat of a CBI enquiry against dad, and I remember mom telling me of dad spending many, many sleepless nights. The CBI coming knocking at your door isn't at all a pleasant proposition for an honest, straight forward employee in a Public Sector Undertaking. He also feared a summons from the Public Accounts Committee, a committee constituted and working under the purview of Parliament. The remit of the committee is to go into the financial statements of Government corporations, Public Sector Undertakings and the like.

Being Felicitated After Calling it a Day at CEMCA After Eight Fruitful Years

The Director Finance was just using the CBI and PAC threats to keep dad on tenterhooks, all the while knowing that he was above reproach and above board. In these difficult times, dad found a very unlikely friend, who was a generation younger, and almost my elder brother's age. The person I am referring to is Mahesh Krishnaswamy, who joined ETTDC with a brilliant academic record, having completed his Engineering from IIT-Madras, and a Management program from India's premier management institute, IIM-Kolkota. He became Dad's close friend, and would drop in occasionally to share a meal with us. He was a very good cricketer, a voracious reader, and had a roaring sense of humour. He would crack jokes on the goings-on in office, and he would have dad and all of us in splits. These were the only pleasant memories that dad took from ETTDC. I think Mahesh left ET & T three months after dad's bad days had begun. And he always used to address dad as CS (an acronym for Company Secretary). Theirs was a lifelong friendship that lasted till my father's last breath.

The CBI and PAC bogey were hung over my dad's head by the Director Finance like the proverbial sword of Damocles. He knew my father's innocence, but seemed to derive derisive pleasure in seeing my father under duress. And sometime in 1982, my father moved on to his last PSU assignment, Educational Consultants India Ltd. (Ed.CIL) as Company Secretary. This company was into the business of educational consultancy, doing projects for their clients who wished to set up educational institutions. It was during the time 1985-86 that Professor G. Ram Reddy came to the office of Ed.CIL, seeking their consultancy services in setting up the Indira Gandhi National Open University. Prof. Ram Reddy was the erstwhile Vice Chancellor of Osmania University, and he was given the mandate by the Central Government to set up a National Open University, named after the former Prime Minister Indira Gandhi.

It was during these visits and discussions at the office of Ed.CIL that Prof. Ram Reddy got to know my father and his professional integrity, and his insatiable appetite for work. He then offered Dad the post of Registrar (Administration) of Indira Gandhi National Open University. My father took the offer, and resigned from the services of Ed.CIL, the last PSU that he worked for.

Setting up a National Open University from ground up was a daunting proposition, and Prof. Reddy found an able ally in dad. We shifted from MIG flats in Prasad Nagar to a five-level duplex accommodation in Asian Games Village in South Delhi. Dad would be buried with work. His working day in office would be spent attending meetings, and all his work would come home in two black leather boxes. He would be already up and working on his files in the drawing room when I woke up in the morning, and I would see him working on his files late into the night when I went to bed. He was to work under two Vice Chancellors of IGNOU, the first being Prof. Ram Reddy, who retired midway through dad's tenure, and was succeeded by Dr. V. C. Kuzhandaiswamy.

While working under the latter Vice Chancellor, dad seemed under constant stress and strain. His telephonic conversations with the new Vice Chancellor would be almost apologetic. Dad was a stickler for doing his work to perfection, and he would leave no stone unturned in ensuring that nobody could pick holes in his work. But in spite of this, there seemed to be an air of uneasiness in my father's interactions with the new Vice Chancellor. Things came to such a pass that midway through his full tenure of eight years at IGNOU, dad wrote out his resignation and handed it over to the Vice Chancellor. And here too, the tone and tenor of dad's resignation letter was taking blame on himself, and not coming up to the Vice Chancellor's expectations. By a strange act of Providence, the

Vice Chancellor, in a rare moment of grace, talked my father out of it, and returned back the resignation letter. Possibly, he realized that without dad, he could hardly get work done in the University. On 30th June 1994, Dad attained to superannuation, and retired from the services of IGNOU. In a rare moment of candour, I remember my father telling me that he must have put in twenty years of work in the eight years that he got to work at IGNOU. That's the measure of the man, and his absolute commitment to his work.

The Loyola College Alumni Get-Together at Rashtrapathi Bhavan with the most illustrious Loyolaite, the then President of India, Dr. R. Venkatraman

He wasn't completely done yet. IGNOU was a member of the Commonwealth of Learning, based out of Vancouver, Canada. The Commonwealth of Learning was contemplating setting up a Commonwealth Education Media Center for Asia (CEMCA) in New Delhi. And they wanted a capable person to head their Finance and Administration. The Commonwealth of Learning had come to know enough about dad's capabilities during his tenure at IGNOU. His new innings post-retirement at CEMCA lasted a good eight years, and it was in the latter half of 2002 that he decided he had had enough, and called it a day.

This post-retirement opening came as a blessing to dad, as it helped him bolster his retirement savings that weren't significant till then. At the time of his retirement, IGNOU hadn't rolled out a pension scheme for its employees. So, his accumulated PF balance, gratuity, and leave salary at IGNOU together amounted to his retirement savings, which wasn't much, and along with his earnings from his time at CEMCA, he thought he had covered all his bases. But from the high-interest rate era of the nineties, interest rates nearly halved, and fast galloping inflation put paid to all his calculations, and dented his savings. But in his nearly fifty years of sincere, committed and honest work, and even in his retirement days, I didn't even once hear my father say with bitterness that for all the work that he put in, he never got duly rewarded for the same. For him, his work was its own reward. He was grace personified, satisfied with his lot in life, and followed in the footsteps of his Araadhya Shri Ram.

A Father Steps Up

After my career had achieved a certain level of stability, there was a certain development on the personal front, which isn't at all easy to overcome. I am referring to unrequited love. I loved a girl who happened to be a good friend of mine, but never ever broached the issue to her for the fear of losing a friend. And even in these matters, I never hid anything from my parents. And when the fateful day dawned, when my feelings weren't reciprocated, with the girl taking the stand that she never had such feelings for me, it was very difficult to stomach.

I broke the news to Dad and Mom, and they tried to counsel me saying that its fine if it didn't work out, but that I must keep my options open to marriage, and that they will do their part in looking for a suitable girl for me. Even after giving them this unfortunate news, there was no bitterness or bad blood from either of them. They were grace personified, and were trying to pull their son out of a trough, from which getting out and remaining positive and graceful is a daunting proposition.

In such situations, the one who is unsuccessful in love very often goes down a downward spiral, wallowing in worthlessness and self-pity. I could well have gone down that road, but for mom and dad's timely and graceful intervention, and Divine Grace that helped me tide over this rather difficult phase in my life. Parents often don't have to preach to their children, but by their conduct set an example for their children to follow. Gracefully dealing with any situation in life, however difficult and insurmountable it may look at first sight was a lesson that stood me in good stead not only in dealing with, and coming to terms with unrequited love, but also developing a certain even mindedness in dealing with this personal setback. I effectively closed that chapter of my life with no regrets, and never again turned back, but in the same vein continued to be a good friend, as I was before.

Possibly, the values that my father ingrained in me through cricket were also to play an important role in coming to terms with this difficult phase in my life. The Spirit of Cricket talks of the highest standards of sportsmanship, and upholding the finest traditions of the game, irrespective of victory or defeat. And as I shared earlier, I loved playing a game of cricket, never obsessed about winning, or fearful of losing. And maybe, it is this phlegmatic attitude that helped me move on from this rather difficult time. And I plied my trade in cricket as an off-spinner. And metaphorically speaking, I didn't have the good fortune to bowl a maiden over. As in the glorious game of cricket, so also in the game of life. And I doff my hat in a tribute to both.

I chose to remain a bachelor, a decision that was difficult for both mom and dad, but which they nevertheless learnt to accept and respect.

A Mentor

This is one of the very important roles played by my father. A mentor to his children, a mentor to his youngest brother, a mentor to his maternal cousins, and mentoring his colleagues in office. And his mentoring left a significant impact on every person he got to mentor.

Beginning with his family, his mentoring began early when we had reached an age to understand the world around us. We were growing up in the era of the Command-and-Control economy, when the State had a role in almost every sphere of business activity, and perpetual shortages of essential commodities was very much the norm. In the late-sixties and early-seventies, even milk wasn't available in the open market. You either had to have a card or a token, and based on the number of members in one's family, a certain quantity of milk would be rationed. One had to wake up pretty early, and place one's milk bottle holder in queue, and then come back a little later when the milk van would offload the milk bottles at the milk booth designated for our locality. I still have vivid memories of my elder brother walking up early between 4:30 and 5:00 am to keep our milk bottle holder in queue, and would go back an hour later to get the milk. Though he was in high school, this was a task that my father had delegated him to do.

As we moved to Delhi in 1975, it was time for me and my sister to step up, as my brother had stayed back in Hyderabad with my uncle to continue his college education. Transfer of the Gas Agency across cities involved the source Gas Agency issuing a transfer receipt, which needed to be produced at the Gas Agency in the destination city. Since everything was done manually, this process would take a couple of months. And till this happens, the fallback measure was to cook using a kerosene stove. The Ration card issued to Dad at Delhi would designate the Petrol Pump from where we had to procure our quota of kerosene. We were staying in East Patel Nagar, and the designated Petrol Pump was at Pusa Road, a good 1.5 – 2.0 kms away. So, I and my sister would be off in the hot summer sun, walking to the petrol pump, getting the kerosene, and taking turns carrying the kerosene can back home. There was no mollycoddling from either mom or dad, and they felt that it was time that their daughter and younger son learnt the ropes of doing household chores.

My sister now took on the role of buying milk based on a token (a flat rectangular aluminum contraption with Dad's name written on it issued by Delhi Milk Scheme). The saving grace for my sister was that the milk booth was bang opposite our house, but getting up early, particularly in the cold Delhi winter wasn't an easy proposition. I remember her wearing a sweater, and wrapping a shawl on top of the sweater to go down to buying milk. She and I also used to go down together to buy vegetables.

It was only when Operation Flood under the able stewardship of Dr. Varghese Kurien who headed Amul that plentiful availability of milk in the open market became a reality sometime in the summer of 1976. The Mother Diary booths had come up in Delhi, and milk would be dispensed using a vending machine, and for every token inserted into the slot, it would dispense half-a-litre of milk. Finally, the spell of milk shortages was broken, and it took a while before milk availability was no longer a problem in all the major cities of India.

When it came to academics, my brother needed no mentoring, as he was brilliant in academics. When he completed his graduation in B.Com in 1978, having stood third in Osmania University, Andhra Bank gave him a direct offer of joining them as a Grade B officer. My brother was very much in favour of taking this career opportunity, but this is where Dad's role as a mentor for him stood out. He counseled my brother saying that a job can wait, and that he should pursue the Chartered Accountancy program from the Institute of Chartered Accountants of India (ICAI). He asked him to come to Delhi and pursue his Chartered Accountancy program. The CA course was a trial by fire for the best of minds. The examination papers would be very difficult, and there would be a compulsory question that everyone had to attempt. The difficulty with the compulsory question was that it would be very difficult to comprehend, and if anyone didn't attempt the compulsory question, his prospects of clearing that paper would fade significantly, even if he/she had fared well in the other questions. The way the syllabus was structured, and the number of groups one had to clear in both CA-Intermediate, and CA-Final was a daunting proposition for the brightest of minds.

My brother given his academic brilliance and acuity of mind didn't disappoint father. He cleared all his groups in the first attempt, barring one paper in one group in CA-Final. And here too, the book he was looking to buy and read from to prepare for his Cost Accounting paper wasn't available in the market. It took Prentice Hall of India a few months to bring out the Eastern Economy Edition of the book, and once it was available, he procured the book, devoured it, and cleared the Cost Accounting paper and the group, securing very good marks in the Costing paper, and in the process, successfully completing his Chartered Accountancy program.

My sister just before the onset of exams in her final year of graduation, applied for clerical cadre posts advertised by the National Bank for Agriculture and Rural Development (NABARD). She cleared the first hurdle of successfully clearing her exams, and the next and most important hurdle for her was to clear her interview. Here, dad stepped in and started mentoring and coaching her on how to face the interview, how she should introduce herself before the interview panel, the prospective questions that were likely to be asked et al. Every evening after returning from office, he would spend a good amount of time with my sister, updating her on current affairs and general knowledge. And she didn't let my father down, successfully clearing the interview, and the first among our siblings to join service. My brother was to join Indian Oil Corporation – Assam Oil Division at Digboi a couple of months later. She went on to do very well in her banking career, finally retiring from service as Assistant General Manager. Dad and I attended her farewell, and dad also spoke at the function. Even at 88, he looked sharp, and spoke fluently and confidently.

Regarding me, every facet of my personality owes its deep gratitude to dad. I had dwelt at length earlier on the many important roles that he played at different stages in my life. And every intervention of his, and his guidance only propelled me forward.

Coming to his youngest brother, he took on a very important role at a crucial time in my uncle's academic career. By this time, dad had finished his education, started his career at AG's Office, Chennai, had put in four years of service, before quitting his government job, and opting instead to move to Hyderabad to take up employment in a private company in order to pursue his academic ambitions of studying Law, and later on Company Secretaryship. My grandmother, though intrepid and a woman of great practical wisdom, felt that my uncle after completing his Pre-University Course (PUC) should take up employment, as she was financially constrained.

It was precisely at this juncture that dad stepped in, convincing my grandmother that my uncle will study, and that he will take on his educational expenses. After completing his graduation in A. M. Jain College in Chennai, dad asked him to come over to Hyderabad. Initially, my uncle had a short stint in Hyderabad Chemicals and Fertilizers, and then when the Reserve Bank of India put out a job ad for clerical cadre posts, my father asked him to apply for the same. My uncle got selected in RBI, and from there ensued a long and fruitful career in banking, first with the Reserve Bank of India, and then moving on to NABARD when RBI decided to hive off its Agricultural Credit Division into NABARD. Even today, when he gets an opportunity, my uncle never misses up a chance to highlight how crucial a role dad played in his life. In fact, uncle used to say that dad almost was like a father to him.

When it came to mentoring his cousins and his nephews, not only did he help them in securing gainful employment, but also opened the doors of his home for them to come and stay with us. I have already mentioned how a couple of his colleagues whom he mentored broke down on the day they came to see him off at the railway station after his stint in ECIL. This trend continued, and he mentored and guided quite a few of his colleagues when they joined Indira Gandhi National Open University. One of his colleagues at IGNOU, who attended dad's cremation ceremonies referred to dad as his father figure.

One specific instance stands out. Dad mentored a friend and colleague, one Mr. S. Guruswamy, who initially started out as a stenographer, and seeing the potential in him guided him to further his academic qualifications. He was very intelligent, and started completing one academic program after another in his chosen field of Personnel Management. He even stayed with us for around 8 months during our East Patel Nagar days, and blazed new trails, finally rising to the position of Executive Director at National Minerals Development Corporation (NMDC). Dad used to affectionately address him as Guru, and uncle Guruswamy is family to us.

A few qualities that are required for a mentor are willingness to share his knowledge and experience, be patient and empathetic, and also provide a roadmap for his mentees. And my father exceeded himself on all these parameters. Finally, a true test of a mentor is to give his mentee wings to fly. And dad did it with panache, as each and every person he mentored went on to soar high in their chosen profession.

For me apart from dad who actively mentored me, another person who silently mentored me was my mother.

An Inspiring Husband

There is a custom in Hindu marriages, wherein the father of the bride puts her hand in the groom's hand to the accompaniment of Vedic hymns. The bride and the groom then go round the Homam (sacred fire) seven times, referred to in Sanskrit as Saptapadi. My mother placing her hand in Dad's was symbolic of the complete faith she put in him in all important matters and decisions that he took concerning his career and family. In the seventh round of the sacred fire that serves as a divine witness, the couple pray to God for companionship, togetherness, loyalty and understanding between them.

A Young Man of Ambition Ready to Take on the World.

And as a child growing up and watching my parents, theirs was almost a lifelong friendship that bravely stood up to and overcame the vicissitudes of life. I have heard my mother speak with a lot of pride regarding the inherent nobility of my father. She wouldn't complain either when dad spent long hours at work, and in the process not being able to afford quality time to family. She took everything in her stride, putting the interests of her family first. And during her final days when she was bedridden, the first person she would send for was dad. Such was her implicit faith in my father.

Mom and Dad Entering into Holy Matrimony (30/06/1955)

As he made career changes that would cause displacement to the family, necessitating our move to a different city, and bringing with it logistical challenges of packing all your things, unpacking them, settling down in a new home; all these didn't faze my mother. She would immediately buckle down to the challenge of setting up her new home, and would start cooking from almost day one, invariably with a kerosene stove in those days. Those weren't the days of Internet and mobiles, where one could order food online, and have it delivered at your doorstep. One could of course go to a hotel and eat for the initial few days, but even this my mother wouldn't do, practicing thrift, and all the while realizing that there was a single earning member, whose salary had to be carefully managed.

Mom and Dad (22/11/1962)

After mother passed away, Dad would often reminisce with a lot of affection and pride, saying that my mother never made any demands of him to tickle her vanity. No expensive jewelry, and no expensive silk saris for her. And this he said made his task of balancing the family's budget relatively easier. And he told me not once but many times that but for the unstinted support from my mother, he wouldn't have gone on to achieve all that he did in his career. And that is a big tribute to my mother.

My eldest Mamaji was older to my father by eight years, and his letters to mom and dad would always be addressed as "My Dear Noble Narayan and Angelic Saroj". At that time, I would think that this kind of address was over the top. But as I look back at the exemplary lives that mom and dad lived, they deserved every bit of this exalted address by my Mamaji. And this was corroborated by a conversation that I had with my cousin Arun (my eldest Mamaji's second son), who told me that Mamaji would tell Arun that he has never seen someone as noble and truthful as Narayan (that is how he addressed dad). And that Narayan and Saroj were a couple made for each other.

A Happy and Rooted Middle Class Family (22/05/1967)

Dad was a firm believer in the traditional religious rituals, and mother would join him in the successful observance of these rituals. But in independent conversations within the family, mom displayed a libertarian streak that questioned the rationale, or rather the lack of it in observing many of these traditions. The true democrat that dad was, he never ever shut her down, or stopped her from expressing her point of view. His expansive heart always had space for a dissenting point of view.

And as the age difference between mom and dad was just a year and a couple of months, theirs was almost a deep and abiding friendship. And mom being blessed with a wonderful sense of humour would occasionally take digs at my father, and the remarkable thing about these situations was that dad would have a hearty laugh along with all of us.

In conclusion, all I can say is that theirs was an ideal relationship that young and aspiring couples would do well to emulate.

An Inspiring and Respected Family Elder

It's a general observation in most families that when it comes to relationships with extended families, there are some for whom we have a special corner in our hearts. And with others who don't happen to be in our chosen circle, we end up just being formal with the niceties, without any corresponding feeling of warmth accompanying them. And this mode of choosing some, and being neutral or indifferent to others is almost a given in familial and social contexts.

Juxtaposed with this was my father whose generosity and affection extended unconditionally to friends and extended family alike. This was his defining trait that was to endear him to each and every member of his extended family circle. Their tone would drop just a shade to convey the respect all of them had for him. And Dad had this remarkable quality of changing his wavelength to the person in front of him, and engage with him/her in a fruitful and meaningful conversation.

Its common amongst families that one who has had an ordinary academic record, and a commensurate career to go with it would generally be ignored, or made fun of. Not only the person concerned, but this condescension wouldn't be lost on his/her family as well. Even these not so fortunate amongst the family invited the same love and affection from dad. One of my cousins who came with this kind of unwarranted baggage has a daughter who is academically brilliant, and is gifted in the fine arts (music and drawing). It was Mother Nature's way of compensating for the unfairness that her family has had to endure. Her daughter got through into one of the leading Engineering colleges, and for which she had to shift base out of Hyderabad. So, she came to call on dad along with her mother before leaving.

And here is where I will talk of another endearing quality of dad. His heart would swell with pride on seeing any child excel in academics, whether within the extended family, friends, or even domestic helps. He would congratulate them, bless them, and give them guidance. So, when this cousin of mine came calling, dad asked me whether we should give some reward for my cousin's child in recognition of her brilliant performance. I asked him to just go ahead, saying he needn't even have asked me. He then took out a gift cover, put a certain quantum of money that was far beyond his modest means, and gave it to my cousin, saying she could use it for buying text books for her child. At that moment, it didn't dawn on me as to the gratitude that she had for Dad's wonderful gesture.

After dad's passing, she wrote one of the finest tributes to dad, saying he was the only one who would send her family a New Year's greeting card (this was before the era of electronic cards and social media). And that she still treasures each of those cards that dad had sent. Her precise tribute to dad was, "A man filled with nobility, compassion, soft-spoken, and the purest soul I have known". Need I say more about my dear father. And she was large hearted enough to extend an invitation to me to the temple town where she stays, saying visiting the many abodes of The Divine that dot this temple town will not only give me solace, but also act as balm for my deep sense of loss, and the ensuing desolation and loneliness.

This tribute from her more than encapsulates the kind of respect and admiration that dad had from family, friends, colleagues and the society at large.

He also helped our domestic help with substantial financial contributions for three academic years for her elder son, and what warmed his heart no end was the fact that the domestic help's boy was doing exceptionally well in his Engineering discipline. And this boy would affectionately address dad as granddad. On important festival days, our domestic help would bring both her boys to pay respects to Dad, and in turn get his blessings.

He read a lot, kept himself cued into the technology developments that defined the era of the nineties, and the first decade of the new millennium. He became computer-literate, had his own email account, and would use it to stay in touch with family and friends. After the passing away of mom, he got books on learning the Kannada language. He was eighty-seven at that time. Such was his zest for learning.

One more endearing quality of his was his disarming simplicity. He would use the bicycle to run errands, when I was working, and not always available at home to attend to household chores. And he rode the bicycle till he was seventy-eight. He never had any false sense of pride that a man of his learning and professional achievements shouldn't ride a bicycle, or do household chores. He would always help mom in the kitchen by cutting vegetables for her, or kneading the dough for making rotis. And he was very adept at making rotis/paratas.

Till he was eighty-eight, he would wash his own undergarment with his own hands. No task for him was too lowly, or below his dignity. He didn't have to lecture to his children about inculcating good values, and always staying grounded.

Rather, he and mom set an example as to how nobly and purposefully one should lead a good life. For children, parents represent a microcosm of the world outside, and they unconsciously emulate the values/behaviour that they see their parents display on a day-to-day basis. Fortunately, for all three of us (rather two as my elder brother is no more), dad left us on a strong wicket, and strongly rooted.

When he was seriously ill from October 2022 – February 2023, one of my very good friends called in to enquire how dad was doing. After she had hung up, dad enquired as to who had called. When I gave dad her name, he spontaneously said, "I have one more daughter enquiring about my health". Whoever reads this paragraph will immediately know as to who this tribute was intended for. Here was a man who doted on his only daughter, but didn't hold back in appreciating the fine gesture of my friend by referring to her as his second daughter.

For him, the whole world was his family, and he lived the Upanishadic teaching of "Vasudaiva Kutumbakam" (the Sanskrit phrase that translates to as "The World is my family").

An Exemplary Karma Yogi

Dad placed the highest importance and value to doing one's duty. His commitment to his duty, or his calling was unflinching. When he got involved with his work, he would literally be impervious to the world outside. During his ET & T days, his office was located in Malcha Marg, Chanakyapuri in Delhi. And on many days, he would come home late from office. His route involved coming through the Ridge Road, which even in the seventies didn't enjoy a good reputation, and people would refrain from traveling through Ridge Road at night for fear of safety. I distinctly remember the days in 1978 when my brother would be out of station on audits as part of his CA articleship, and my sister after her studies for the night would fall asleep. Mom, unable to bear her anxiety would wake me up, and I remember keeping vigil along with mom from our second-floor balcony waiting for dad to return home.

While I was battling my examination phobias in my senior secondary school days, dad would counsel me to take courage and face exams head on. In one of those counseling sessions, I remember him telling me something that still rings in my ears, even after the passage of a good forty-three years. His precise words were, "Son, even if you have to die doing your duty, don't flinch, but rather do it".

Dad had been in the NCC during his school and college days, and therefore, when the call went out from the Army for young men to volunteer and join the Army in the light of the 1962 war with China, dad immediately went to the Secunderabad Cantonment to join the Army. He didn't think about his career, or his family (my brother was five years old, and my sister just 6 months old). The war was ending, and therefore, the prospect of dad joining the Army never materialized. That's patriotism for you. When he used to wish me on birthdays, his firm handshake always had the aura of a handshake from someone from the Armed Forces.

And now I dwell on a different type of courage, an inner courage that is far more important in dealing with life's setbacks, of which my father had more than his share. In the year 1963, my paternal aunt (the only sister among the five siblings) passed away owing to childbirth complications. All the brothers doted on their only sister, and the telegram that informed of her passing away completely shattered dad. In fact, I see two images of my grandmother, photographs taken of her during the time when my aunt was alive, and photographs after her passing. While the former photographs presented a healthy image of my grandmother, the photographs of her after the passing away of my aunt show my grandmother as a pale shadow of her former self.

In the year 1967, when my sister was just five years old, she contacted TB Meningitis. There was an error in diagnosis, and by the time it was diagnosed, the tuberculosis had affected her brain, which makes a child give out a cry referred to in medical parlance as a meningeal cry. My youngest uncle who was staying with us then distinctly remembers the scene of dad carrying the limp form of my sister in her arms to the hospital, barely able to hold back his tears. She was admitted to Niloufer Hospital, a government-run hospital for children. Fortunately, in those days, very good doctors used to work for these government hospitals, and there was an excellent pediatrician, Dr. Dikshit who used to attend to my sister, apart from other children in the hospital. That was the time when the antibiotic streptomycin had come into the market as an effective antibiotic for fighting TB, and she was in hospital for a month along with mom, who took care of her ailing child. With timely medication, rest and good food, my sister bounced back to good health in a matter of six months. Our family doctor, Dr. K. S. Rao, used to refer to my sister as a medical miracle, saying TB meningitis generally affects one of the faculties such as hearing, or seeing. But my sister got away mildly, having to wear spectacles for some time.

Now, we fast forward to the year 2001. It was late-December. It was 29th of December precisely. My brother's eldest son, who was born in the year 1989 with a genetic disorder that later got diagnosed as mitochondrial disease, was confined to bed all his life. But the child was a beautiful soul, which captured the heart of anyone who came in contact with it. He was a child of ethereal beauty, a beauty that touches your soul. The doctors didn't give the child more than a dozen years, and it was in fact after he had completed twelve years that he passed away in the wee hours on a cold wintry morning on 29th December 2001. He had passed away in his sleep.

This was the first death in our family. His passing left everyone in a pall of gloom and grief. I was not in Delhi with them at this time, having moved to Hyderabad. It was a dull Saturday morning when something didn't seem right for me. And my unease stood vindicated when dad called up, and broke down on the phone informing us of the passing away of his grandson. While the rest of the family was shellshocked, the cremation rituals had still got to be completed. Understanding the grief of my brother and my sister-in-law, my father took upon himself the task of bathing his grandson's body, draping a white dhoti around his body, and applying the religious mark on his head, a defining characteristic of followers of Sri Vaishnavism.

This must have been a heartrending experience for a grandparent, but he bore it all with his trademark fortitude.

A decade after this untimely death of a young child came the passing away of my elder brother, who was battling renal failure for close to a decade. He had fallen back on his only option, which was to opt for dialysis sessions twice a week. But renal failure imposes severe dietary restrictions, mandating a low-salt, low-potassium diet. Water consumption also had to be strictly regulated. And this disease slowly wears down the patient, and that is what happened to my brother. A handsome man in his prime was reduced to a shadow of his former self. Beginning December 2010, he was in and out of Apollo Hospital, Delhi, and from mid-January 2011 to mid-February 2011, he was in hospital for almost four weeks before he was discharged. He was yearning to see his second son, who was autistic, and therefore, hospitals weren't too accommodative of allowing specially-abled children. He came back home on the 16th February, spent a day at home on the 17th, and breathed his last in the wee hours of 18th February (Brahmamuhurtham time of 4:00 am on a full moon day). My father was in Delhi to be of help to my brother's family, and when the dreaded phone call came on 18th morning at the unearthly time of 5:00 am, I knew something was wrong. The landline phone used to be in our parents' bedroom, and before I could pick the phone up, mother had already picked up the phone, and dad in a completely broken state conveyed the news of my brother's passing to my mother. My mother though initially badly shaken, regained her composure, as stoicism was her defining trait. I and mother along with uncle and aunt left by flight to Delhi. As my brother's son was autistic, it was decided that he should not do his father's last rites, and that lot fell on me.

There is a saying that nothing teaches you more detachment than a visit to the cremation grounds. And it is not totally unfounded. As I lit my brother's funeral pyre, the beginnings of my learnings in detachment had well and truly begun. It doesn't happen overnight, but is a process that plays out over a period of time. In that fateful moment dawned the realization that nurturing one's ego, harbouring perceived slights and wrongs from others does not amount to anything but a fistful of ashes.

On 8th December 2019, mother had a fall in the kitchen. I was away in Abu Dhabi conducting a training program, and in fact, was on my way back that very same day. After touching down, I called home and dad answered the call, giving me this bad news. He said that he is proceeding to the hospital, and asked me to come straight to the hospital. Dad had in the meantime, with the help of an auto driver in our colony and our domestic help's husband, managed to get mother on to an auto and took her to the hospital. X-Rays and MRI revealed a fracture of her right humerus, and also a fracture of one of her lumber vertebrae. She underwent successful surgery for her right humerus, but the doctors didn't attempt any surgery for her fractured vertebra given her age, instead advising complete bed rest.

But as is generally the case with senior citizens who have a fall, and are advised complete bed rest, complications start arising, and so it was with my mother's case. As the nurse at home was doing nothing more than giving my mother her sponge bath, and giving food and medicines in a timely manner, we felt shifting her to a rehab home would be a better option, as it promised physiotherapy, counseling, and constant round the clock attendance by doctors and nurses. Moreover, she had started declining food, and on 22nd February, she even declined water.

I spent the first three nights as my mother's attender at the rehab home, before dad took over on the 25th February. It was fitting that dad was with my mother when she breathed her last in the early hours of 27th February. Sister had come down to stay with me, and she slept in my parents' bedroom. The fateful ring of the landline phone at an early hour got us apprehensive, and I think my sister took the call and received the news of mom's passing. We immediately rushed out, took the metro train to Ameerpet, and from there took an auto to the rehab home. Dad, I and my sister brought mother home in an ambulance.

Dad's companion of sixty-four years was gone, and yet after overcoming his initial grief, he set about guiding me on the modalities of conducting my mother's cremation. He first asked me to visit the cremation grounds, and book a slot for mother's cremation in the evening. And then he in turn informed our family priest, asking him to come down and conduct mother's cremation ceremonies as per Hindu custom.

I would digress slightly to relate a tale to my readers. Once a sage was passing through a town, and everyone rushed to get his blessings. The sage blessed one man who had gone to take his blessings with these words, "You should die first, followed by your son, and then your grandson. The man was taken aback at this rather strange blessing, and mustered up the courage to ask the sage as to why he blessed him thus. The wise sage told him, "Do you want it to be otherwise?". The man at once understood the wisdom of the sage's utterance. It is the ordained order of Nature that older ones leave first followed by the younger ones. But when the sequence is reversed, it can be a curse to the family elder, seeing his child, and grandchild go before him.

For us, it was nothing short of a curse, and more so, for mom and dad who had the mortification of seeing their grandchild (my brother's eldest son) pass away, followed by the death of my brother. This is where I see a distinct parallel in the trajectory that life took in both my father's life, and that of his idol Lord Rama. In a way, Lord Rama's life was marked by one tragedy after another, which he faced with stoicism, courage and fortitude. And my father, followed in the footsteps of his idol, braving setbacks and tragedies that struck him one after another with courage and fortitude. There must have been a lot of sadness inside him, but he never showed it.

To sum up, he was an exemplary Karma Yogi, who carried out his duty, and left the rest in the hands of The Divine.

Down But Not Out

Beginning July 2011, Dad had to undergo an annual procedure called Endoscopic Retrograde Cholangio Pancreatography (ERCP) for insertion of a biliary stent into his narrowed biliary duct, referred to in medical parlance as a biliary stricture. I would accompany him for the procedure, pay up the money, and await our turn. Dad would then be wheeled into the endoscopy suite, and this entire procedure would be done under sedation. He would undergo this procedure at the Asian Institute of Gastroenterology (AIG), under the able and efficient care of Dr. Manu Tandan. After the procedure, Dad would be discharged as an outpatient, and we would be home.

Dad would have a light dinner to negate the nauseating effects of sedation, and he would be on an antibiotic dosage for five days, after which he would be back to normal. This process would play out annually without any problems till the year 2022. All the while, in the preceding years, the doctor would tell me that long-term stent usage will have some impact on his liver.

Beginning August 2022, dad's intake reduced. He would complain of bloating, and would cite lack of appetite for his reduced intake. This continued till end-September of 2022. In these two months, dad also experienced gut leaks, with mucus and stool coming out along with gas. Finally, on 7th October, we went to see the gastroenterologist Dr. Manu Tandon at AIG, who put him on an antibiotic dosage for ten days, and asked us to see him thereafter.

On 17th October 2022 as we were getting ready, dad suddenly exclaimed that his trousers weren't fitting him. It was then that a painful realization dawned on me. My brother used to complain that renal failure leads to fluid retention in the body, particularly the stomach, causing his trousers to tighten. Since June 2016, dad was also being treated for declining renal function, as was evidenced by his serum creatinine levels gradually climbing to 3.3, way above normal. So, I asked dad to wear a dhoti and a shirt, and we set off in an auto to see the doctor. The doctor physically examined my father, and after pressing his stomach, said that fluid had accumulated in his abdominal cavity, referred to in medicine as Ascites.

Dad's urine output had also declined, and we also had to see the urologist at the Asian Institute of Nephrology and Urology (AINU). The doctor said that dad will have to undergo an ultrasound scan of his urinary bladder once before passing urine, and have the scan again after passing urine. The objective was to find out residual urine in his urinary bladder. Dad underwent the scans by waiting it out at AINU, and I had to switch between AIG and AINU. Fortunately, my cousin was with me, and he was with dad, while I rushed to AIG to see the gastroenterologist. The doctor had an air of pessimism about him. And when I pressed him as to what can be done to address the problem of Ascites, he told me that they could tap out the fluid from his abdomen, but the tapping shouldn't be done frequently, as it would open the risk of infection, and given my father's age (he was eighty-eight then), the doctor was apprehensive. The doctor said that fluid accumulation could be due to infection, the most common being tuberculosis in India. The other reasons for it could be declining liver function, pancreatic cancer, or even declining renal function. He was not outlining any clear line of action, and I don't know what made me ask the doctor the question. "How much time do you give my father?". The doctor said that given the state of dad's liver and kidneys, and also his age, he gave dad not more than six months. Anything above six months would be a bonus he said. My heart sank after hearing this news. He said that dad could be prescribed a diuretic to drain out the fluid from his abdomen, but high doses of diuretic couldn't be prescribed given his renal problem. He could prescribe the dosage only after hearing from his nephrologist.

I had to rush back to AINU, and the urologist after seeing dad's ultrasound scans didn't have good news either. He said that dad's urine output was low, given his longstanding prostate problem, and said that dad had to be on a urinary catheter. So, a urinary catheter was placed, and a bag attached at the other end for urine to collect in the bag, which had to be periodically emptied.

I along with my cousin and dad returned home at 6:30 pm. And he sat at the dinner table and had his dinner. And I didn't realize then that it wasn't until after the passage of five months that he would return again to the dinner table and have his food. I distinctly remember the day. It was 19th October, and I think it was evening. Dad had gotten into the state of being bedridden. Mucus and stool had leaked out and Dad asked me to clean him. I had got all the necessary things for this: cotton, gloves, disinfecting solution et al. There was no sense of revulsion, as I readily put on the gloves, took a small wad of moistened cotton, and cleaned Dad's anus.

This was a defining moment in my evolution as a caregiver for dad. I had taken to being his caregiver seamlessly without any inhibitions. Dad started complaining of backpain, probably due to the accumulated fluid in his stomach putting pressure on his back. On 26th October, I called on Dr. Tandan to ask him whether dad could be admitted to AIG, and he asked me to get dad admitted on the 27th morning. After admission, the doctor advised his team and nurses to tap out fluid from dad's abdomen, and nearly 3.5 litres of fluid were tapped out.

His stent replacement was long overdue, having been delayed due to the onset of Covid, and on 29th October, Dr. Tandan successfully performed an ERCP for removal of his old stent, and replacement with a new biliary stent. The doctor also did an endoscopy of his esophagus to check for any infection, and fortunately for dad, the result was clean, implying no infection. All the while, multiple tests were being done to determine whether dad had tuberculosis. One of the TB tests check for ADA (adenosine deaminase) levels, and the ADA levels were borderline negative, implying no tuberculosis. On 31st October, dad was discharged, and asked to report again after ten days. On 10th November, I again took him to AIG, got him admitted as an inpatient, albeit for a day, and again two liters of fluid were tapped out.

It was at this juncture that the doctor took a realistic call. He said that ADA levels being borderline negative implied an 80% probability of tuberculosis, and instead of surgical incision to take out tissue from his stomach, and then do a biopsy for TB that could be painful for dad given his age, he relied on the probabilistic chance of TB being there, and started TB medication to be taken for a minimum period of six months. The medication started around mid-November, and this is when dad's health issues started increasing. His food intake had dropped significantly, probably because of the liver not functioning optimally, and also because of the plethora of medication that he was taking; for his kidneys, liver, and now TB medication.

A month-and-a-half into his illness, dad developed bedsores, one in his tailbone area, and also one each on both his buttocks. I got cotton, betadine, and ointment to clean and dress the bedsores, but I realized that dad experienced pain whenever he tried to sit up in bed. It was then that I decided to shift him to Yashoda Hospital, Malakpet, for I realized that his bedsores needed more professional hands than my amateur attempts at providing relief. Upon admission, standard tests were prescribed, which revealed low platelet count, and low hemoglobin levels. The nephrologist and the gastroenterologist told me that low platelet count and low hemoglobin levels were not isolated occurrences, but rather a manifestation of his malfunctioning liver. A malfunctioning liver also affects the clotting mechanism, as was evidenced from his bedsores, which were bleeding. The gastroenterologist told me that it was mandatory for dad to have his bowel evacuation every day, and prescribed Duphalac for the purpose. He said that metabolites need to be pushed out of the body. Otherwise, metabolites remaining in the body can cause mental confusions. Little was I to realize that this problem was to confront me for the better part of January 2023.

While being treated by the plastic surgeon for his bedsores for which he used some special kind of dressing that I was seeing for the first time, and which he said facilitated faster healing, he was also given a unit of plasma and a unit of blood to improve his platelet and his hemoglobin count. After spending three days in the hospital, we returned home on the 3rd of December. But rather than show an improvement, his condition on the contrary started deteriorating. The strong anti-TB antibiotics killed his already very low appetite, and his food intake was restricted to almost a semi-solid or fluid diet. The plethora of medications created constipation for dad, and he had lost so much of weight and become so weak that he didn't even have the strength to push out the hard stools.

There was a particular instance when I took him to the bathroom for his bowel clearance, and after some initial effort, part of the stool had come out. Dad didn't have the strength to push it out completely. It was then that I embarked to help him, which I clearly attribute to The Divine giving me the strength and the wisdom to do so. I put on surgical gloves, and pulled out the hard stools that dad was finding it difficult to push out. This wasn't something that I was doing of my own volition. I had become an instrument in the hands of The Divine, and I just carried out the will of God.

In hindsight, I don't think dad had TB, for his body was reacting very strongly to the TB medication. He would frequently throw up even fluids like coffee and beverages. After five weeks of TB medication, seeing his condition, I and my sister who had come down to help me decided to stop his TB medication.

In the early morning of 1st of January, 2023, Dad vomited dark vomit, and it scared the wits out of me and my sister. Later in the morning, I spoke to Priya, my cousin sister, who is a doctor in the US, and she based on my account didn't give too bright a picture. All this while, during the preceding two months, dad would hardly sleep well, moaning all night, unable to withstand his physical suffering. The doctor therefore gave him a pill to enable him to sleep well. Even the small dosage was so strong for him that he was kind of sedated for most part of the day. I remember calling on his gastroenterologist, and updating him of the happenings on the morning of 1st January, and based on my account, the doctor kind of concluded that dad was in the pre-terminal stage, and that I can stop his medication, keep him comfortable, and that I could start informing his near and dear ones.

Only I and my uncle were privy to the doctor's observations, and we chose not to share it with anybody in the family, including my sister. After waiting for more than a week, around the 15th of January, I asked dad whether he would be ok to stop all his medicines. He was ok with my suggestion and immediately said yes. I was taking this decision in consultation with his doctors. But his mental confusions were to surface for the entire month of January, adding another layer of worry to his already frail physical condition. Some very old memories of dad would resurface in the current context. For example, my grandfather had a gramophone which my father distinctly remembers, and regrets that elders in the family didn't make an effort to save it as a family heirloom. So, the gramophone would come back to the present, and he would say that he saw it just on the double bed in his bedroom, and would ask me where it was. Or the barking of stray dogs in the neighbourhood would make him hallucinate those dogs had entered our home. If I tried to negate him by saying that nothing of that sort had happened, he would get angry. So, I learnt a very important lesson. I would just hear him, and slowly change the conversation, and his mental hallucinations would slowly subside.

The nephrologist at Yashoda Hospital, in order to help my father sleep better, and also to overcome his pain, recommended a pain patch called Buvalor pain patch. It is a medicated transdermal patch, wherein the medicine would act subcutaneously through the skin. I put the patch on his shoulder blade, and he started to sleep well. But his mental hallucinations didn't seem to relent. Later on, I realized that Buvalor pain patch was a mild medical narcotic, and suddenly I realized that this could also be contributing to his mental confusions and mental hallucinations.

The day was 3rd February 2023. It was a Friday. I spoke to Priya (my doctor cousin) regarding the new information that I had gleaned about Buvalor pain patch, and asked her whether it could be contributing to dad's hallucinations. She told me that she was about to tell me the same, and advised me that if dad was sleeping well, and wasn't encountering any pain, I could take the patch off. After hanging up, I asked dad whether I could remove the pain patch. He readily agreed. I gently removed the Buvalor patch, and thoroughly cleaned the shoulder blade with a wet wipe where it had been placed.

The weekend 4th and 5th February passed off uneventfully. Then on the 6th morning, he woke up a new person. A great majority of the mental confusions was gone, barring one-odd confusion which I learnt to assuage by the doctor writing on his file that there was nothing of the sort that he was visualizing, and that he was well.

All this while, every three weeks beginning October 18th, his urinary catheter had to be changed. And after being treated for bedsores and being discharged, one of the nurses at Yashoda Hospital was graceful enough to volunteer her services for dad. She would come home every three weeks to change his catheter, and would come once a week to clean the bedsores which were healing, and put new dressing of the same specific variety that the plastic surgeon had used in the hospital to dress his bedsores.

He had a catheter change on the 12th February, and we went to see the urologist on how long the catheter had to be used. He was pleasantly surprised when he saw dad, and said that he looked much, much better than when he had seen dad on October 18th. When he came to know that the catheter had been changed just a few days back, he deferred the Cystoscopy he was planning to do, as doing a Cystoscopy would mean removing the catheter, and the same catheter once removed, isn't put back. He asked us to see him in the first week of March.

On 7th March, we reported at Asian Institute of Nephrology and Urology for our appointment with the urologist. He conducted a cystoscopy, and a test more, and then laid the options on the table. The doctor didn't recommend the conventional procedure Trans Urethral Resection of Prostate (TURP), as it involved a laser to trim the enlarged prostate, and which would be done under general anesthesia. Given dad's age, he instead recommended a new procedure call Urolift that was non-invasive, didn't warrant general anesthesia, and would use slings to secure the enlarged prostate on either side of the urethra, thereby reducing pressure on the urethra, and allowing for the free passage of urine. The doctor was honest enough to tell me that the Urolift procedure was more expensive than the conventional TURP procedure. I reassured him that that was fine, and that we will go with the Urolift procedure.

The procedure was scheduled for the morning of 13th March 2023. We entered the hospital on the evening of 12th March to complete the admission formalities. The next morning, Dad was wheeled out of his room for the procedure. After the completion of the procedure, he was moved to the surgical ICU, and I was given permission to see him. He told me that the procedure was painful as it involved the application of only a local anesthetic. Dad's pain threshold was pretty high, and it was this coupled with his grit and courage that made him endure the pain during the procedure. The catheter was put back, but this time only for a couple of days.

The doctors said that some amount of blood along with the urine was normal for the first couple of days, and that gradually, it would lessen, as would be evidenced by the color of the blood in the urine getting lighter and lighter. Dad was in hospital till 14th March, and on 15th March 2023, dad was discharged from hospital, more importantly without a catheter. This would have made a huge psychological difference to dad, as having a catheter and carrying the urobag everywhere could be mentally disconcerting, and dad had stopped entering the pooja room at home because of this.

After nearly five months of disuse, dad had to retrain his bladder muscles once again, which took him a few days. At this juncture, I had come to know that vitamin B1 strengthens the nerves that control the bladder muscles, and with the doctor's permission, I got a bottle of vitamin B1 tablets. He started taking these tablets once a day, and within a couple of weeks, his urinary output and urinary function was back to normal.

Dad had beaten the conventional viewpoint that once a catheter is put, it never comes off. I just had no rational explanation to this miraculous turn of events that began on the 6th of February 2023, and culminating with his return to normal by late-March 2023. The only reason I could ascribe for dad's miraculous turnaround in his health was Divine intervention. No doctors. No medicines. No nothing. The Divine had orchestrated a miraculous comeback for dad.

The Divine Lends a Helping Hand

In the months of December 2022 and January 2023, when Dad's health had hit a nadir, in order to make him feel better, I would sit by his side on his bed, and recite the Sri Vishnusahasranamam. Even in his agony, with his eyes closed, whenever I would lose track of the next shloka that I needed to recite, he would give me the cue for me to resume my recitation of the Sri Vishnusahasranam. Such was his implicit faith in The Divine. And during this time, he requested a picture of Sri Rama, Divine Mother Sita, brother Lakshmana, and Hanuman to be shifted from our pooja room to his bedroom. Lord Rama was his idol, and I am sure the presence of that picture in his room gave him spiritual and mental strength.

And when during these two months, dad showed no signs of improvement, I would get very despondent and have an internal dialogue with God that went thus. "God, here is my father, a man of God, who put his entire faith in your grace, and has withstood all tragedies in his life with grace and fortitude. My father returning to good health is not my father's test; rather it is Your test to restore him to good health." Such was my defiant dialogue with The Divine during these difficult times.

Why God made him suffer for five months before orchestrating his near miraculous recovery is something only

God can answer. I cannot venture into speculating answers where I don't know anything.

I think the date was 22nd March 2023, the beginning of Chaitra Navratri. It would culminate on the 30th March. This was the time of the celebration of the Divine Mother. And on the 9th day of Chaitra Navratri was Ramanavami, the birthday celebrations of Lord Rama, dad's idol and inspiration. Having his bath daily and saying his prayers was something central to his routine. And this had got disrupted from October 2022 – mid-March 2023. A few days before 22nd March, I had decided that beginning 22nd March, come what may, I will ensure to give dad his daily bath, so that he is mentally at ease before beginning his prayer routine. And what began on 22nd March 2023 was to continue till 3rd December 2024.

The winter of despair had well and truly ended. And the spring of hope and rejuvenation had begun for dad, thanks to Divine intervention.

Turning a Nonagenarian

Dad started making progress as the summer of 2023 approached. He had lost a lot of weight, and had lost muscle tone and strength. He was prescribed physiotherapy and exercises, and a physiotherapist came home to teach him exercises to bring back some amount of muscle strength and muscle tone back.

Sometime in June 2023, I suggested to dad that he take Ayurvedic medicines from Kotakkal Aryavaidyashala for his liver, and kidney issues, and also his hemorrhoids problem, which had started troubling him of late. It wasn't something new, and which he had from his mid-forties, but the problem had become a little more difficult to bear. Dad was a stickler for following the doctor's prescribed dosage, whether allopathic or ayurvedic. He started taking ayurvedic medicines. And one of the good things to come out after his Urolift procedure at AINU was that one of the doctors attending on him, who was an endocrinologist said that dad needed to take his medicine for his sugar problem only if the sugar level crossed 200, not regularly. The same applied to his blood pressure medicine, to be taken only when the blood pressure registered an increase, and not regularly. Apart from these, a lot of other medicines that he was taking for his kidney problem were gradually stopped, as they tended to cause him lot of gas.

So, he was on minimal supportive allopathic medicines for liver and kidney function, and ayurvedic medicines. But in spite of staging a remarkable recovery, dad wasn't the person of old anymore. His movements were measured, and his gait had slowed down, but he was mobile enough to move around at home. Excursions out of home had been ruled out. I had got him a quadripod walking stick, and this gave him the confidence to move around the house without any apprehension.

The only visits outside home would either be a visit to my sister's place, or my uncle's place for important family occasions, or a visit to the temple that he loved going to. I remember taking him to the Skandagiri Temple in Secunderabad, the abode of Lord Murugan. This was the temple that I had visited in December 2022 when dad was seriously ill.

I would take dad for his quarterly reviews with both his gastroenterologist as well as his nephrologist. They would review his blood reports, which were reasonably alright. But some of his liver parameters had long been a concern. Due to his declining liver function, his albumin levels were way below the normal range, for which the doctor had long been asking dad to start eating eggs. Dad being a strict vegetarian pushed back to the best extent possible. As the months of 2023 rolled into 2024, we realized that it was a very important year for all of us. For on the 25th of June 2024, dad would complete 90 years.

Sometime in April 2024, after his regular quarterly review with his gastroenterologist, the doctor suggested that it was high time that his biliary stent was removed, as it was nearly eighteen months since the stent was last inserted in October 2022. In the first week of May 2024, dad got admitted as an inpatient, albeit for a day, and using the same ERCP procedure, Dr. Tandan removed the old stent. But this time, he did not insert a new stent for two reasons. First, the biliary stricture or narrowing had opened up, and second, he didn't want to insert a new stent, because when the time came for its removal, dad would be a year older, and the doctor opined that dad may not be able to withstand the procedure. I fully concurred with the doctor's argument, and we returned home.

Turning a Nonagenarian

There were no side effects of non-placement of stent, and so I guessed dad was doing well. In June, I and my sister started drawing up plans for celebrating dad's ninetieth birthday celebrations. Both of us got a collector's edition of The Bhagavad Gita for dad, and my sister also suggested we buy clothes for dad on this momentous occasion. We got some fine dhotis and kurtas for dad. And dad readily accepted my suggestion that each of the attendees at his ninetieth birthday celebrations receive a silver coin of Goddess Lakshmi from him. I met one of the leading jewelers in Hyderabad. He had readymade coins of Goddess Lakshmi, and he put each of the coins in a nice round box, before putting it in a pouch. And we decided to keep it a family affair, with my sister's family and my uncle's family joining in. We decided to book a restaurant called Sattvam for dad's birthday dinner, specifically for the reason that Sattvam served only Sattvic food, that is food prepared without onion and garlic. Dad had taken initiation from our spiritual preceptor sometime in 2009, and since then, had stopped eating onion and garlic.

My sister's children brought a garland for their dear grandfather, and also got a cake to be cut by dad for the occasion. After the cake cutting and gifting was over, we all sat down to have our dinner, and it was after a very long time that the extended family was sitting together and having food. Dad ate little but relished the food there. I attended to his specific dietary requirements by getting him food that was mildly spiced, and which his digestive system could manage. After the dinner, dad gave each one of the attendees the silver coin of Goddess Lakshmi, and blessed them.

Both I am my sister felt very happy that we had the good fortune of celebrating the 90th birthday celebrations for at least one of our parents. Dad too felt very happy at the pleasant turn of events, and we all returned to our respective homes a contented lot.

Silent Transmission

Now, I am going to dwell on the most important aspect of these nearly two years of taking care of dad. Being his caregiver was a transformative experience for me. In the initial stages of his illness during the period October 2022 – January 2023, I struggled to adopt the new routine of being his caregiver, as I had never before been exposed to this role. I learnt my ropes of being his caregiver with active support from my sister, and my uncle and aunt who had come down to be of moral and material support during these testing times.

As I had alluded to earlier, I pleasantly surprised myself by easing into the role of being my father's caregiver. While I was able to do this, managing the home, and making special preparations for dad which could agree to his weakened state was a responsibility that my sister carried out with aplomb. With her help, I slowly started making all this a part of my regular routine. This wasn't an onerous task for me simply because I didn't have a large circle of friends, who I would miss once I became my dad's caregiver. I was basically an introvert, and had gotten used to living my life without friends. It wasn't as if I shunned them, but they always seemed frightfully busy managing their careers and their families. So, my transition to being dad's caregiver was natural, without me having to give up on meeting and going out with my friends.

Taking care of dad brought me up close with human mortality. Old age doesn't spare anyone. I knew a day would come when I too would suffer the infirmities of old age as dad had suffered during his time of illness. This realization dawned pretty early, and I realized that as a son, it was my moral duty to attend to my father in his old age. People around me started commending me for what I was doing. This left me a little surprised, for I was doing nothing extraordinary, but just doing my duty to my father.

Dad's training early taught me that when I was faced with a crisis, like the illness of a loved one, the first thing is to keep your emotions in check. For getting emotionally upset clouds your reason and judgment, and once that happens, it becomes very difficult to take good decisions. And that is what I did when dad fell ill. I just kept my emotions in check, and did what was required of me in the given moment.

As parents grow older, they generally start getting the feeling that they are becoming a burden on their children. To ensure that dad never got this feeling, I started a practice that I continued for close to a year. Every night, before retiring, I would give dad a hug, and he in turn would embrace me with a lot of love, and bless me. There were occasions when he would do a gentle head butt with me, the ones that we do with little children. These were days of emotional and spiritual enrichment, which no money on earth could buy. And I wouldn't trade these emotional and spiritual riches for a king's ransom.

Being my father's caregiver taught me lessons in patience, empathy, compassion, and perseverance. These lessons really sunk in and wrought an inner transformation in me, which I never had imagined so far in my life. It made me a far, far better person than what I was before my father's illness began. This was an education that not even the finest educational institutions anywhere on earth could give. I have said this many times to a couple of my close friends, and I would like to say it again for the benefit of my readers. I consider the two years of being dad's caregiver arguably my finest work to date in my life. Academic achievements, professional achievements all look insignificant before the work of being dad's caregiver for two years. There were certainly occasions when I would lose my temper at dad. But I would be the first person to apologize to dad, and he would make light of it saying he didn't take it to heart.

There were many an occasion dad would tell me as to what he would have done without me. On one occasion, I told him that God had sent me specifically to attend to my ageing parents. Being a bachelor was certainly a big help, as the burdens and cares of looking after my own family wasn't there for me, and I could devote my energies full time to attend to my ageing parents. The fact that I called time on my career in December 2015 seemed a good move, for it enabled me to attend to my mother in her last days, and I just couldn't imagine how I could have taken care of dad if I had continued with my career. Companies wouldn't indefinitely allow you leave of absence to attend to an ailing parent, and I thanked God that he gave me the wisdom to call time on my career at just the right time, as it gave me the bandwidth to be a full-time caregiver to my dad.

In the Indian spiritual tradition, there are umpteen instances where the Guru and the disciple just sat face-to-face with their being no verbal interaction between them. And yet in that profound silence, the Guru transmitted whatever he had to, to his willing disciple. The foremost of these examples is that of Lord Shiva sitting in rapt meditation, and his seven disciples who are popularly known as the Saptha Rishis waiting to receive Lord Shiva's grace. It is said that the Saptha Rishis sat in rapt attention before Lord Shiva, eager to imbibe his teachings. After a very long period of waiting thus, Lord Shiva happy at the sincerity and commitment to learning of his

Saptha Rishis, began transmitting the science of Yoga to them, and entrusted them with the responsibility of spreading it far and wide.

Right from childhood, one singular observation that I made was that mom and dad were never given to moralizing or pontificating to their children. By their exemplary conduct in thought, word and deed, they set a personal example for their children to follow, and evolve into good human beings.

These two years of taking care of dad were an apprenticeship in man making that I underwent under dad. He never gave me any teaching, or any parental advice. There was a profound silence. And in that silence, the lessons that I had to learn got transmitted from dad to me. It was as if Destiny, Providence, or Existence had willed this important, silent transmission of wisdom, that kneaded, shaped, and chiseled me into a far better version of myself.

Passing into Eternity

This is by far the most difficult chapter to write for me as it details the weeks and days leading to my father's demise. But this is an important part of his life's narrative, and it must be told to the readers with as much objectivity as I can muster.

From the latter half of July leading to the first week of August, I noticed an unusual swelling of his legs, not the typical swelling of the feet, but a swelling of the legs from knees upwards. Starting with the knees the swelling extended to his thighs. I had been noticing it when I used to give him his bath. And we knew that a visit to his gastroenterologist was mandated. The doctor saw him, and immediately diagnosed the swelling in his legs to hypoproteinemia, a condition characterized by low protein in the body, and in my father's case, caused by declining liver function.

The doctor said that dad could come in as an outpatient, and they will intravenously give him three units of albumin, and also a gram of iron to improve his protein and iron respectively. But that would mean visiting the hospital on three consecutive days, and waiting in the Emergency area to get treated, which given dad's frail health wasn't the most desirable place to be waiting, as I feared that dad might catch a secondary infection there. I therefore requested the doctor to admit dad as an inpatient, and do the needful.

We entered hospital on the 13th August, and he was given one gram of iron and one unit of albumin intravenously.

And not more than a bottle of albumin could be given intravenously in a day. So, we had to stay in the hospital till the 15th of August. Two more units of albumin were administered intravenously on the 14th and 15th August. And during these three days at the hospital, I found dad struggling physically. The surgical cot even after allowing for hydraulic adjustments and being brought down to its minimum height was such that when dad tried to get down from the cot, his feet were still a good two feet away from the floor. A wooden block was provided but putting both feet on it would cause dad to lose his balance, and I had therefore to ask him to put one foot on the wooden block, while lowering his other foot on the floor. It then became easier for him to move his foot from the wooden block to the floor and get up and walk. Getting into the washroom was again a challenge as the floor of the washroom was a good foot above the floor of the hospital room.

And the western commode seemed pretty old, of some local make, and poorly designed. The commode's height was pretty low, and with some help from me and holding on to the grab bar, dad would manage to sit on it. But after finishing his bowel routine, it was really difficult for a ninety-year-old man to get up from such a low height. I am not physically well endowed, and not a man of even reasonable physical strength. But I still endeavoured to put my hands under his arms, and try to help my father get up from the commode, which was a daunting proposition given my lack of physical strength. On one occasion, while helping him get up from the commode, I very nearly overbalanced and fell, just managing to keep my balance. This created a slight apprehension in me as to whether this was going to be the new normal once we reached home. On the evening of 15th August, dad was discharged from the hospital. After we came home, to my great relief, dad was able to get up from his cot on to the floor as the cot was pretty low compared to the surgical cot in the hospital, and unlike the hospital, the floor of the attached bathroom in dad's bedroom was at the same level as the bedroom floor.

And from the 5th of August, dad started eating eggs, realizing that this was possibly the only way he could improve the albumin levels in his body. The doctor advised him to eat three egg whites, and half a yolk. Dad started eating three egg whites along with his breakfast of two slices of bread toast, and his strength levels registered a gradual improvement. He was also put on a minimal dosage of diuretic to drain out the fluids accumulated in his legs.

We would still occasionally visit out sister's place, and in September, we even made a visit to our sister's place on the occasion of the birthday of my brother-in-law, and from there went to my uncle's place to call on aunt who wasn't doing too well. Dad would get a bit tired after returning home, but nothing untoward in his health surfaced giving any cause for concern.

He had his Liver Function Test, and Renal Function Test one last time on 25th October, and everything seemed ok, as parameters need to be interpreted relative to the age of a person. Sometime, in November, I would notice that dad would get up in the night to pass urine a couple of times, and the time it would take him to finish his routine and settle back into his bed seemed inordinately long. I would sleep in my room, and being a light sleeper, would see the light in his room for much longer than usual. Dad didn't tell me, nor did it occur to me that he was slowing down.

Beginning the second week of November, dad had trouble steadily holding the coffee tumbler in his hand, and on a couple of occasions, it would slip from his hand and land on the table. I saw this even with the glass of water that would be kept next to his plate during lunch or dinner. The beginning of the third week of November saw my cousin sister and her daughter calling on dad. She was on a visit to Hyderabad from Chennai, and took this opportunity to call on dad. I had a pictorial book of Albert Einstein that I wanted to gift the child. As was his wont, Dad volunteered to giftwrap the book. He had gift wrapping paper always stocked at home, and was an expert in giftwrapping. But on that day, he struggled to gift wrap the book, and managed to do it with great difficulty.

His handwriting which was steady, and greatly admired in the family also became unsteady. He was in the habit of writing his diary every day. And I could see that he struggled to keep his hand steady while writing. He was also very conscientious in daily recording his health parameters and medicines that he was taking in his diary, and all this was becoming a struggle. He complained of tremors in his hand, and I took him to our family physician, Dr. A. Jayachandra. The family physician noticed a slight slur in Dad's speech, saying it could be caused by transient ischemia in the brain. He suggested an MRI of the brain for dad, and even if something showed up, he said that little could be done given my father's age, and that he was not very much in favour of prescribing the medicines for treating this problem.

I was apprehensive of taking dad for an MRI, for the technician at the lab told me that dad would have to be still in the MRI machine for at least fifteen minutes. Dad's hearing loss was a little more pronounced at this time, and he couldn't wear his hearing aids when doing the MRI, as metal objects aren't allowed when doing the scan, and I knew dad would have trouble hearing instructions from the technician.

On the 26th of November, I took dad to a neurologist, hoping that the neurologist would have a better solution to dad's problem. He said dad seemed a little stressed for want of proper sleep, and prescribed him two medicines Prolet-25 to help him sleep better and a multivitamin. I even checked with the doctor whether the dosage was low given dad's weak constitution, and he told me that he was giving him the minimal dosage to be taken twice a day.

He took one tablet of Prolet-25 on 26th November, and two tablets a day for the next four days from 27th – 30th November. From the 29th November, I would notice that he would have his bath, and I would help him apply the religious mark of Sri Vaishnavism on his forehead, as his hands weren't steady. But instead of sitting for his prayers, he would wish to lie down and sleep. He would be deeply asleep, and it would take me quite a while to wake him up to have his lunch. On 29th and 30th, this sleeping became even pronounced, and it would take me at least ten minutes to wake him up. He would have a little bit of food, and would rest again.

Two lines of thought were going through my mind. One was whether the medicine prescribed by the neurologist was causing dad to sleep like this. So, on the 1st of December, after giving him one tablet of Prolet-25 in the morning, I checked with both our family doctor and my doctor cousin in US about continuing this medicine. Both of them were unanimous in their counsel to stop this medicine.

Since my family doctor had a very busy schedule, I started checking with my cousin whether dad sleeping like this was a sign of his bodily systems gradually shutting down. She said it could also be the reason. Beginning 26th November, his gait had slowed down significantly, and I would ask dad to put one of his arms around my shoulder, and help him move within the house.

Till the 3rd of December, dad still religiously followed his daily routine. He would have bowel clearance, have his bath, but was unable to say his morning prayers. On the evening of 2nd or 3rd December, I gave him his prayer book from which he would read out the shlokas, just to keep him engaged. He sat on the chair, and it looked to me as if his eyes and his mind weren't active. He hadn't moved past the index page of the book for a few minutes. Sensing my mistake, I asked him to put the prayer book away, and rest if he so desired.

Beginning 26th November, I started sleeping in my father's bedroom just to help with his nocturnal visits to the bathroom. I would wake him up once in the night to empty his bladder. The reason was that it would take him time to get up from bed, and walk slowly to the bathroom, and a filled bladder would make it difficult for him to hold the urine in his bladder, as bladder muscles weaken with age.

On the intervening night of 3rd and 4th December, both I and father had slept off, and when I opened my eyes, I saw that it was 5:00 am in the morning. His night visit to the bathroom hadn't happened, and therefore, I woke him up. He got up very slowly and walked to the bathroom to ease himself, and also clear his throat, as he had caught a cold. After clearing his throat, he was unable to walk the 6-8 steps to his bed. I was holding him from behind, and I just didn't know what to do at that hour. My phone was on the cot, and I had to leave him in order to move to the bed to reach my phone. But I was fearful that leaving him alone might cause him to fall. So, I cajoled him to take one baby step at a time. Slowly but surely, he managed to walk those few steps and reached his bed. I changed him into fresh clothes, and he maneuvered himself into a sleeping position of his own.

It was at this moment that this painful realization came to me that making dad go through his daily routine was now fraught with a lot of risk. I got up, and went to prepare coffee for myself and dad. My cousin sister in a conversation the day before had suggested a home visit by a doctor to medically assess dad. After my morning routine was done, I went out to see whether any doctor would be gracious enough to come home and do a check up of dad. I was out by 10:00 am, and surprisingly many of the clinics in our area hadn't even opened for the day.

I managed to find an ayurvedic doctor who was gracious enough to come home and examine dad. He prescribed some ayurvedic medicine that he himself had, but I didn't want to give too many medicines to dad without consulting our family physician. On the afternoon of 4th December, he skipped lunch and had a few sips of his favourite beetroot-carrot juice. In the evening, I messaged our family physician regarding dad's cold, and he prescribed Paracetamol 500 mg tablets. I had to interject and tell the doctor that Dad was having trouble swallowing small tablets in the past few days, and swallowing a large 500 mg tablet was certainly not on. I then told the doctor that I would give him Paracetamol syrup of the same strength instead. In the evening, my sister and my brother-in-law came calling. My sister wasn't keeping well, and dad ventured to ask her why she came to see him when she herself wasn't keeping well. As they were taking leave of dad, he asked me to see off my sister and my brother-in-law till the gate. As evening transitioned to night, I wanted dad to have one teaspoon of the Paracetamol syrup, and asked him to eat something before his medication. He again took a few sips of beetroot-carrot juice before taking the medicine. He was conscious, and asked me to come and sleep by his side, as I had had a busy day. After settling down in bed at around 10:00 pm, dad started coughing a lot. I therefore got up close to midnight, woke him up and gave him a teaspoon of Dabur Honitus, an ayurvedic cough syrup. This was going to be the penultimate time he was going to be conscious.

His coughing continued through the night, and started subsiding as morning approached. I didn't wake him up, as he had a restive night, and wanted him to sleep for some more time. After preparing coffee for both of us, and after completing my morning routine, I tried waking him up, but he just wouldn't wake up. It was as if dad had gone into a deep sleep. One of my cousins, Ramesh asked me to arrange a home visit by a doctor from Apollo Home Care Services, a reputed name in health care in India. I arranged for a home visit by a doctor from the panel of Apollo Hospitals, who came to examine dad on the evening of 5th December. He examined him with a stethoscope, and wrote out a prescription in which he had prescribed tests, and also wrote out an antibiotic called Augmentin, along with dextrose and saline drip, all to be administered intravenously. He took a picture of his prescription on his phone and told me that the corresponding teams from Apollo Home Care would come to take his samples, and a nurse would come and stay back to administer the antibiotic, dextrose, and saline solution intravenously.

I had sounded off my cousin brother (my uncle's son) about dad's declining condition, and he had taken a flight the previous evening to fetch my uncle and aunt who had gone down to Trichy to spend some time with their eldest daughter. They arrived in Hyderabad on the 5th evening, and my cousin drove them straight home to look up dad. My father wasn't responding to the calls of my uncle and aunt as well.

The nurse from Apollo Home Care came around 9:30 pm. He was a guy in his late-twenties, and I asked him about the equipment, to which he said that his supervisor would get it. The supervisor came a little letter with just a backpack, and when I asked him about the IV stand, he said that he didn't bring it. I then asked him how he was going to administer the medicines and the saline and dextrose solution intravenously without an IV stand. He started talking of some makeshift arrangements, and I put my foot down, saying that he either administer the medication following proper protocol, or doesn't do it at all. In a conversation in the evening with the very same supervisor, I had clearly asked him to get whatever he needed to treat father at home, and that I would reimburse him for the same.

The IV stand came close to 11:00 pm, and the nurse's supervisor asked me whether I had a suction machine at home. He had just got a nebulizer along with the other consumables. At that time of night, where would we go looking to buy a suction machine. They set up the IV stand, and Augmentin, dextrose and saline drip started being administered intravenously to dad. While this was on, the nebulizer was applied, and by close to 1:30 am of 6th morning, the saline drip finished, and it was time to retire to bed. I asked the nurse whether he would sleep next to dad, to which he said that dad's guttural noise created by his breathing (I thought phlegm in his chest was causing this sound but it was something more serious as the doctor was to tell me on the evening of 6th December) wouldn't allow him to sleep. I found this reply rather strange, and took pity on the thorough lack of professionalism from a nurse from Apollo Home Care. I asked him to sleep on the divan in the hall, and I slept next to dad.

My uncle and aunt returned to their home after seeing dad, but my cousin stayed back with me. Both of us were unanimous in our opinion that Apollo Home Care was a disaster waiting to happen, and more or less decided that we will move dad to a hospital once it was day. In the morning, dad continued to sleep without responding to our calls. My cousin sister from San

Diego was on phone, and my cousin brother was talking to her. In the course of her conversation, she said that for someone like dad who was very weak and not even awake, it was mandatory to apply suction using the suction machine immediately after nebulizing so that the phlegm in the throat could be sucked out. This wasn't done the previous night. The nurse was again preparing to give the nebulizer to dad without following it up with a suction machine, and once my sister gave me this critical information, I stopped the nurse from proceeding with the nebulizer. In response to my queries to Apollo Home Care as to when they were going to send me the suction machine, Apollo started sending me payment links for purchasing the suction machine as well as the oxygen concentrator on rent.

My cousin was on a video call, and she wanted to see dad in the video call. She saw him breathing heavily, and she asked me to request the nurse to check dad's oxygen level. When I asked the nurse to do the same, he said that he didn't have an oximeter. This was the proverbial last straw on the camel's back, and was proof of the thoroughly unprofessional services of Apollo Home Care.

My cousin brother had already spoken to Care Hospitals, Banjara Hills for sending an ambulance to shift dad there. I spoke to our family doctor, who was the Director of Pulmonology there. He asked me to send him a short video of dad, and after seeing it told me that dad was in the pre-terminal stage. He had in fact asked me earlier to take care of dad at home, as he said that hospitals are not very receptive to age-related cases. He was possibly setting my expectations at a very realistic level, and I responded to him by telling him that I also kind of understood the grim situation, and wanted my father's last days to be pain-free and under professional medical care, which is possible only in a hospital. I even explained to him my disastrous experience with Apollo Home Care. And I assured him that I will stand firmly with him in any decision he took regarding dad, as we have known him for twenty-five years, and he was family to us.

He then asked me to bring dad straight to Emergency Care at Care Hospitals, Banjara Hills, and that he would inform Emergency Care of the same. And he advised me to say NO to Emergency Care asking me to put dad on a ventilator. The medical emergency ambulance came at around 10:00 am, and dad was immediately stretchered into the ambulance. I sat next to dad along with the nurse. She was an efficient nurse, who immediately applied suction machine to remove phlegm from his throat. This was while we were enroute to the hospital. My cousin brother sat in the seat adjacent to the driver.

Dad was immediately ushered into Emergency Care, and doctors immediately started checking his vitals. Blood samples were also taken, and a doctor there asked me about dad's health background, which I fully gave to her. In the late afternoon at around 3:30 pm, our family physician, Dr. A. Jayachandra came to see dad. He asked me to wait outside while he went in. After a few minutes, I was called in, and Dr. Jayachandra told me that dad's condition was declining, but as a doctor, he couldn't say when it will all end, and that we will have to wait. He then explained to me that the guttural sound that dad was making is referred to in medical parlance as the Death Rattle. This I later checked out is a symptom that shows up a couple of days before the inevitable end. The doctor clearly gave out instructions to all and sundry there that only comfort care needs to be provided to dad, and that there should be no CPR, no resuscitation, no intubation, and no ventilator. Dad had become so weak that if CPR had been attempted, his ribs would have broken. And the doctor took a very wise call ruling out all the aforesaid measures. He also asked the medical team to insert a Ryle's tube or a nasogastric tube, so that dad could get some nourishment.

Dad was moved to his room at around 5:00 pm, and he was put on an intravenous drip, and under constant medical attention of doctors and nurses. The duty doctor told me that they attempted inserting a Ryle's tube through his nose, met with resistance, and didn't want to push it for fear that it may cause nasal bleeding to dad. I stayed back with dad in the hospital, and on the 7th morning (a Saturday), the doctor came to see dad at around 9:00 am, and asked me whether there was any improvement, to which I replied with a No. He again asked why the Ryle's tube was not inserted. He said if they experienced difficulty in inserting the normal tube, they could try inserting a thinner tube, as he felt that dad needed some nourishment, saying saline drips hardly provide any nourishment. He then left dad to the care of the duty doctors and nurses there, and moved on to see his other patients.

My uncle and his grandson came to see him late in the morning on the 7th, but dad wouldn't respond, and continued with his deep sleep. In the afternoon, one lady doctor managed to insert the normal Ryle's tube skillfully, and then, they wanted to do an X-ray to determine whether the Ryle's tube was positioned correctly in the stomach. By the time all this was done, and the protein feed started, it was late evening. And this feed had to be interrupted in between for his nebulizing sessions as well.

It must have been 9:00 pm on the 7th night. I was having dinner with my back to dad, when I heard dad call out to me "Balu, Balu" in a deep, sonorous voice. I immediately rushed to dad, and assured him that he was in hospital, and that he was under professional medical care. He gestured with his hands to me, indicating that the Ryle's tube be removed, and I had to tell him that that cannot be done, as a protein feed was being given through the tube, and once he got well, it can be taken off. He kept awake for close to ten minutes and after calling me twice, didn't speak further. This gave me some faint hope that he might come through this ordeal.

On Sunday, the 8th December, he continued sleeping and didn't wake up at all. My uncle's eldest daughter flew in from Trichy to see dad. She came to the hospital with her younger son, and tried gently to wake dad up, but to no avail. After they had left, I sat and prayed sincerely to The Divine to end Dad's suffering and to give his soul a peaceful release. There is a large statue of Lord Ganesha in the Reception area of the hospital, and I stood there and prayed to Vignhartha to grant dad a peaceful exit.

As evening moved into night, I kept a sole vigil by my dad's side. Our cab driver, Wahid came late in the night to see Dad along with his wife. They took turns to come and see dad, and by this time, dad's face had taken on an ashen pale colour. I retired at around 12:45 am. I woke up around 3:45 am and went close to dad to see how he was doing. He was breathing, as was evidenced by the gentle heaving of his chest. I returned to my attender's bed, but couldn't sleep as the light in the room was directly falling on my eyes. One light in the doorway of the room is kept on for nurses to come and check up the patient. I turned my face towards the wall, hoping to avoid the light and to get some sleep. But I don't know what made me get up again within a few minutes. Four to five minutes would have lapsed when I woke up again. As I passed the clock in the room, I saw that the hands of the clock were somewhere at 3:57 am. As I neared my father's bed again, I saw that he wasn't breathing, and his head had tilted to his left side. I immediately called out the duty nurses, who came and started checking his vitals, and the readings were erratic. A short while later, the duty doctor came to check on dad. She was the same lady who had seen dad the previous evening, and had patiently answered my questions regarding dad. She waited a few seconds, as she said that she saw faint readings. She then checked him with a stethoscope, and asked for a bedside ECG to be done. The ECG technician came with his equipment, and after fitting the electrodes on dad's chest took his ECG reading. The ECG machine showed the dreaded flat line indicating that dad was no more.

The doctor then set about writing the certificate mentioning the cause and time of death. The time of death was mentioned at 4:13 am, but I knew that he had passed away earlier close to 4:00 am. As per the Hindu calendar, it was the ninth day or Navami thithi, a day associated with dad's idol Lord Rama. And in Hindu religion, the early morning time starting from 3:30 am – 5:30 is considered very auspicious, and referred to as Brahmamuhurtham. My father's soul had cast off its mortal coil in Brahmamuhurtham time on Navami thithi. The Divine had heard my prayer and gracefully put an end to dad's suffering.

With dad's passing, a noble era had come to an end. An era marked by truthfulness, honesty, uprightness, integrity, and total commitment to his duty. A man who lived an ideal life deserved a graceful ending, albeit the four days of suffering he had to endure. The administrative staff and the security officer in the hospital very extremely courteous and helpful. The security officer immediately sounded housekeeping to dress dad's body. The security officer even arranged for an ambulance for me to take dad home. I immediately started reaching out to family informing them of dad's passing away. I called our family priest for conducting dad's cremation ceremonies, and he said that he would come at 3:00 pm.

I left the hospital close to 6:00 am in the ambulance carrying dad. The ambulance driver was smart enough to enquire from me whether I needed an icebox to keep dad's body to which I replied in the affirmative. We reached home at 6:45 am, and the icebox followed suit shortly. Dad's body was placed in the hall in the icebox.

From 9:00 am onwards, relatives started pouring in. My sister's family was the first to come in, and my sister overcome by grief broke down. I had to console her asking her to attend to her indifferent health at that time. Uncle's family came in later. And then my sister-in-law, and my cousins (my father's elder brother's sons) came in to see dad. Other cousins also came in. A little later than 3:00 pm, our family priest arrived, and the preparations for dad's cremation commenced. At close to 4:30 pm, dad's body was shifted to the hearse van, and I along with my uncle and four of my cousins who volunteered to be pall bearers left for the cremation grounds in the hearse van. The priest made me do the necessary rituals before asking me to light dad's funeral pyre.

The next morning, on the 10th December, I had to go to the cremation grounds to collect dad's mortal remains. Our family priest was already there, and made me do all the necessary death rituals for my dear father before asking me to put dad's mortal remains into a small urn. It was gut wrenching to pick the mortal remains of a man I had loved, respected, admired and idolized. The priest consecrated the ashes and mortal remains before asking me to put dad's mortal remains into the urn. The ashes were now ready for immersion into a holy river. And what holier river than Mother Ganga. Dad had expressed his desire to immerse his ashes in the Ganga at Asthi Ghat in Haridwar.

On the 10th afternoon, I booked air tickets for me and my cousin from Hyderabad to Dehradun. From Dehradun, it is a 45-minute cab ride to reach Haridwar. I had planned to immerse

Dad's ashes in the Ganga, and return the same day, i.e., 11th evening. My cousin cautioned me saying I may be cutting it too fine considering the onset of winter, and there being every possibility of flight delays owing to fog. I took the chance and we left on the 11th morning for Dehradun. The flight left on time, and arrived in Dehradun on time. I had already spoken to an acquaintance (a cab driver in Dehradun) to arrange for a cab and pick us up from the airport. The cab was waiting for us, and it was a bright sunny day in Dehradun. We reached Haridwar before noon. I and my cousin reached Asthi Ghat. I changed into a dhoti, and carrying the urn containing dad's ashes, I entered the swift currents of the Ganga. I emptied the urn containing dad's mortal remains and ashes into the holy waters of the Ganga, and prayed to The Divine for his soul to attain liberation, and reach the lotus feet of The Lord. I then took a dip twice in the Ganga. It was as if The Divine had orchestrated this entire sequence with clockwork efficiency to ensure that the immersion of dad's ashes into the Ganga went off without any hitch.

My father, my Maryada Purushottam, had attained the feet of his Maryada Purushottam and his Aaraadhya, Lord Rama. Incidentally, it was the 11th of December, which was auspicious for two reasons. It was Mokshada Ekadashi, and also Geeta Jayanti, the anniversary celebrations of the day Lord Krishna gave his sermon on duty to Arjuna on the battlefield more than 5000 years ago. And I didn't choose the day. Providence had made me do it, choosing a very, very auspicious day to immerse dad's mortal remains in the Ganga. A truly remarkable and glorious life had come to a graceful end.

Epilogue

This then dear readers, is the remarkable life story of my father, my Maryada Purushottam. It is also a story of the making of man; a testimony of how he faced trials by fire early on in his life, and made a man out of himself. Not only that, he made men of many more people, his colleagues, his friends, his cousins and nephews, his youngest brother, and of course his two sons, about which I have written in detail in this book.

And he had prepared me for life after him. In the immediate aftermath of his demise, I kept my emotions in check, and started attending to all the logistical details that are required to arrange for the cremation ceremonies of my father. And this stoic resolve continued as his thirteen-day ceremonies commenced and concluded on 22nd December.

I am sure mom and dad would have worried no end of what would become of me when I was completely lost in my senior secondary school and college days. A young teenaged boy who had become despondent, diffident, and completely lacking in self-belief and self-confidence. Dad showed infinite patience as I floundered time and time again in my graduation till, I somehow completed it, thanks to dad and The Almighty who made it possible. To have turned around such a boy into a confident young man, and preparing and toughening him to fight his battles in life on his own was dad's single most important achievement.

As children, we always yearn to have our parents by our side, providing us support and inspiration. But there comes a time when the bodies of our parents age, making it increasingly more difficult for them to carry on with the business of living. Their souls cry out to The Divine for a release from their ageing bodies. And after shouldering the responsibilities of the head of the family for close to 70 years, he finally cast off his mortal coil for a rendezvous with his Aaraadhya, Shri Ram.

In my nearly sixty years of life that I have lived, I have yet to see someone as noble as my father. And I can say with certainty that in my remaining years, I will not see another like him. To borrow a quote from the Great Bard's play Julius Ceaser, Mark Anthony's tribute to Ceaser could well apply to Dad. **"When comes such another"**.

Dad, you have left behind a huge, irreplaceable void. But you have also given me the inner strength, the courage and the fortitude to deal with it. To strive to lead a life in the manner you lived your life, and to carry forward your precious legacy. This memoir is an attempt to preserve and carry forward your precious legacy.

Pranaams Appa